SEEING THE EASTERN STATES

O come, let us sing unto the Lord;
Let us make a joyful noise to the Rock of our salvation.
Let us come before his presence with thanksgiving,
And make a joyful noise unto him with psalms.
For the Lord is a great God, and a great King above all Gods
In his hand are the deep places of the earth;
The strength of the hills is his also.
The sea is his, and he made it;
And his hands formed the dry land.
O come, let us worship and bow down;
Let us kneel before the Lord our Maker.
For he is our God,
And we are the people of his pasture, and the sheep of his hand.

Psalm 95: 1-7

FOREWORD

FOR the fortunate traveler who plans to journey through the Eastern States by train, by automobile, or on foot, this volume is designed as an aid in mapping out routes, a companion on the way, a reminder of the historic associations from Portland to Pittsburgh and from Niagara Falls to New York, New Jersey and Delaware.

But should the projected vacation journey so carefully planned prove impossible the long summer will seem to loom ahead dark, gloomy, forbidding. Such a vision is so unpleasant that most people are apt to resist the suggestion that they decide to make the best of a bad business and get as good a vacation as possible without leaving home. How can they be expected to find pleasure in a place the resources of which were exhausted long ago?

But have the resources of the square miles near home been entirely exhausted? Has it never occurred to us that there is a possibility of seeing the familiar things in a new way, to say nothing of seeing among them familiar sights that never met our eyes before?

Perhaps the roads and the streams and the trees close to our homes have more to show us and to tell us than we have thought. Let us listen to them, and so be ready for the greater enjoyment of the scenes that are near as well as of those that are farther away. And if there is a time when we cannot even go to scenes around home, let us keep in mind the statement of W. P. James, the English author of the book, "The Lure of the Map," that if he had to choose one work to take with him to a desert island he would take an atlas. The title essay in the volume dwells lovingly on the fascinations of the map. Have you ever tried an atlas as a substitute for an impossible vacation journey? It makes a better substitute than many people would think.

The map should be read in the light of figures—both arabic and rhetorical—like those given by an editorial writer in the Philadelphia *Public Ledger,* concerning a large portion of the territory described in *Seeing the Eastern States*. He told of "that most extraordinary natural division of America known as the great coastal ellipse that reaches from Maine to Maryland, with Portland and Washington as the two foci, and which takes in the lower end of Maine, a third of New Hampshire, all of Massachusetts, Rhode Island, Connecticut, New Jersey and Delaware, with a fifth of New York State, a fourth of Pennsylvania and a half of Maryland. This geographic ellipse, whose backbone is the axis of the "Falls Line," on the geological formation of the continent, is an empire in itself, in which is found not only more than one-fifth of the population of the country, but the most dazzling manifestation of that civilization which the world calls American. . . .

"Within this ellipse is also found a radiant countryside that ranges from the mountains and lakes of New England to the Palisades of the Hudson—compared with which the glories of the Rhine sink into insignificance—and the quieter rural beauties of the rolling country round about Philadelphia. And everywhere throughout this countryside its humanization has added a touch of unusual charm to that which is beautiful in itself and is a challenge to the mere artificially arranged aspects of Old World landscapes.

"Merely to touch the fringes of the significance of this coastal empire is to stimulate the imagination with rarities, since within it are not only found the resources of the New World in glittering superabundance but the rich spoils of the whole earth. It was Kipling who, entering New York harbor on one occasion, saw there, for the nonce, 'the most stupendous loot' man had ever gathered together. But New York, while the culmination, is only part of this coastal empire which, with the capital of the nation within its metes and bounds, determines not only the destiny of America but that of the world."

Then think of adding, to the superb country described by the editorial writer, the remainder of Maine, New Hampshire, New York, and Pennsylvania, and all of Vermont—omitting only Maryland, which has been included in an earlier volume in this series! What an opportunity the territory provides for the traveler, the sportsman, or the seeker after rest!

The author speaks gratefully of help received from many while he was Seeing the Eastern States, including Colonel Henry W. Shoemaker, of McElhattan, Pennsylvania, L. K. Stubbs of West Chester, Pennsylvania, George P. Singer of St. David's, Pennsylvania, and William F. Dawson, of Lynn, Massachusetts. He says "thank you" to Henry van Dyke for permission to use poems quoted in this volume, and to Edward Stratton Holloway for the artistic beauty of the frontispiece.

JOHN T. FARIS

PHILADELPHIA,
    APRIL, 1922.

7

CONTENTS

9

ILLUSTRATIONS

ILLUSTRATIONS

ILLUSTRATIONS

ILLUSTRATIONS

SEEING THE EASTERN STATES

CHAPTER I

FOLLOWING THE RUGGED COAST OF MAINE

FROM Kittery Point to Eastport is only about two hundred and fifty miles in a direct line. But let no traveler deceive himself into thinking it will be such a simple and prosy matter to go from one end of Maine's coastline to the other. For there are more than twenty-five hundred miles of shore line in and out of the bays and inlets, around islands, skirting headlands. The first part of the journey will seem comparatively simple—for from Kittery Point to Casco Bay the cliffs and beaches, while abounding in scenic magnificence, are comparatively sedate. But there is no simplicity in the labyrinth that extends from Portland to the New Brunswick line. To trace a way through this labyrinth even on a detailed map of the coast makes the heart of the lover of the out-of-doors leap. And when comes the long-anticipated experience of following the maze itself, standing on its headlands, crossing to the islands, gazing out to the ocean dotted with sails, then the pulses tingle and the blood seems to course more swiftly.

The Maine Coast begins where the Piscataqua River comes down from Portsmouth among rocks to the sea, divided by the island on which is Newcastle, where the Peace of Portsmouth was signed by the representatives of Russia and Japan. Ten miles out in the ocean are the rocky Isles of Shoals, part of them claimed by New Hampshire, while part give allegiance to Maine. At low tide there are six of them, though at high tide there are eight. The name of the group was given because of great shoals of fish found there by the early visitors. Some of the individual islands have names equally descriptive. Hog Island—called Appledore Island on company occasions—when seen by the approaching sailor, is said to look like a hog's back rising from the sea. Smutty Nose also has a company name, Haley's Island, but the popular title tells of a dangerous black point of rock dreaded by navigators in these waters. The name Duck Island speaks for itself. Square Rock was so named because it is nearly round. Star Island and Seavey's Island and White Island are also in the group.

Summer visitors who cross to the islands from the mainland find relaxation on the rocks and in the caverns, in the old church on Star Island, the scene of the labors of missionaries supported by the "Society for Promoting Religious Instruction in the Isles of Shoals," and in the cemetery where stones erected to the memory of ancient worthies tell of their virtues. There is no lack of employment for vacation days on these barren rocks that look like "the bald peaks of a submerged volcano, thrust upward out of the water."

The easiest route back to the coast ends at the point where the study of the shores should be continued, at Kittery Point, separated from York, Maine—the Agamenticus of early days—by York River. Beyond the

HIGH ROCK, GILEAD, MAINE

PORTLAND HEAD, NEAR PORTLAND, MAINE

river is famous York Beach, and five miles farther on Bald Head Cliff lifts its weather-scarred side far above the surf. The mighty rock withstands the pounding of the waves, but those who feel it tremble beneath them wonder that it is not destroyed.

Many years ago Samuel Adams Drake held that the bit of coast from York to the region of Wells, is one of the finest bits of walking in New England. And from Wells through Kennebunk Beach and Kennebunkport to Old Orchard and Cape Elizabeth, many feel that the way has equal charm.

Cape Elizabeth affords the first prospect of Casco Bay, with rocky Portland Head, crowned by the lighthouse, not far distant. Portland, the city of Longfellow's youth, looks out from its peninsula on the scores of islands in the bay, inviting the visitor to climb the hills at either end of the city and to study houses made famous by men and women of other generations, of course including the house where Longfellow wrote some of his early poems, now set apart as a memorial of his life.

If there is one feature of Casco Bay that deserves mention more than another it is Harpswell Neck, a point of land that reaches out from the mainland toward Portland. A number of islands lie between the city and the village on the Neck which was the scene of the early ministry of Elijah Kellogg, the author of the declamation that most boys have used, "Spartacus to the Gladiators."

In all this region history vies with scenery in its demands on the interest of the visitor. At Brunswick, where Lyman Beecher was pastor of the Congregational Church, Harriet Beecher Stowe had the first inspiration for "Uncle Tom's Cabin."

Near Brunswick is Bath, in a county whose name, Sagadahoc, is a reminder of the days when, in 1605, George Waymouth named the Kennebec the Sagadahoc. The stream was known by this name to two early colonies that settled along its banks, the Popham Colony of 1607, whose members remained at Hunniwell's Point until they grew discouraged and returned to England; and a trading company from the Plymouth Colony which came to the stream to trap and trade. From the gains of the settlement the Pilgrim Fathers were able to discharge the debt they owed to the London Company for paying the expense of the historic voyage of 1620.

Perhaps twenty miles from the site of the ill-starred Popham Colony's settlement is Pemaquid, at the mouth of the Pemaquid River. There a flourishing settlement existed early in the seventeenth century; there Samoset, the friend of the Pilgrims, had his house, and to this place the Pilgrims looked for supplies that saved them from starvation. In 1689 the Indians destroyed the flourishing village. Later Fort William Henry was built so as to include Pemaquid Rock within its walls, and from above the rock the flag of Great Britain floated until the French lowered it in 1696. Another fort was built in 1727, and other enemies came and went before it. Long since, however, enemies passed away, and the peaceful town looks out on the sites of the forts of old, on the beacon light that guides the navigators, and on the basaltic bowlders that show the way to the inner harbor.

18

Ten miles from Pemaquid lies Monhegan Island, which has been called "the most famous island on the New England map." On its seaward side the surf knocks insistently on the rock-ribbed barriers that stretch away for several miles. On the landward side are the quieter waters where, in 1814, the American *Enterprise* engaged the British *Boxer* and won the fight, though the victorious captain was killed and was buried in Portland by the side of his British foe.

Northeast of the site of the sea-fight Penobscot Bay looks out on the Atlantic through its fingers of scattered islands. Some of these islands boast the quarries from which granite was taken for government buildings in Washington as well as for the Brooklyn Bridge and the Eads Bridge at St. Louis.

In the days of Samoset, who traded much of this territory for a few furs, Camden, on the west side of the Bay, was known as Megunticook, a name that persists in Megunticook Peak, 1457 feet high, highest of the Camden Hills, and the most commanding point between Canada and Florida.

Belfast, of shipbuilding fame, is the last of the towns on the west side of the bay that claims Plymouth Colony as ancestor. In 1630 Plymouth granted land for the use of settlers below the mouth of the Penobscot River.

It is said that the Penobscot was the fabled Norembega, told of by early French explorers, which led to a city of barbaric splendor whose site was indicated on an Antwerp map of 1576. Thirty-four years later Champlain sailed for twenty-two leagues up the river, in search of the fabled city. He found nothing but wilderness. If he paused on his way back at Castine,

19

opposite what is now Belfast, he would have seen a view of nobility sufficient to make most men forget a mere disappointment in a sordid search for gold.

From Penobscot Bay the coast line is even more indented than before, because of bold peninsulas, deep inlets and islands of which Mount Desert is largest and most famous.

On the last of these—Moose Island—is Eastport, which just manages to be within the borders of the United States. For years Great Britain claimed the island, though Massachusetts incorporated the town in 1798. Even when the British troops were about to evacuate the island in 1818, the commander refused to recognize Eastport, but insisted on dating his letters from Moose Island, although the replies were dated from Eastport!

Moose Island is nearly five miles long. At one side is towering Todd's Head, several hundred feet high, which reaches out into Passamaquoddy Bay, toward New Brunswick. It shares with West Quoddy Head in Lubec, at the other end of the island, the name "the jumping-off place."

Northwest of Moose Island the St. Croix River enters Passamaquoddy Bay. The identity of the river of this name, mentioned in the Treaty of Ghent as the eastern boundary of the United States, was long in doubt. Great Britian claimed that the St. Croix was a stream farther west; this was her reason for claiming Moose Island. The boundary dispute was not settled until 1831, when the king of the Netherlands, appointed arbitrator between the nations in accordance with the provisions of the Treaty of Ghent, awarded to the

United States seven-eighths of the territory between the boundary desired by Great Britain and that claimed by the United States. If Great Britain's claim had been allowed the territory of Maine would have extended little north of the northern line of New Hampshire.

And ever since there has been peace on the border, as there will surely be peace for ages yet to come.

CHAPTER II

THE ROMANCE OF LAFAYETTE NATIONAL PARK, MOUNT DESERT

IT does not seem natural to speak of a National Park in the East; somehow the words take the hearer in imagination to the West where mountains and lakes, waterfalls and canyons provide fit settings for majestic playgrounds of the people.

Yet since February 17, 1919, it has been necessary to revise such notions, for then President Wilson approved the action of Congress in setting apart as the heritage of the vacation-seeker and the lover of nature the most appealing portions of Mount Desert, the island on the coast of Maine that has excited the wonder and admiration of visitors, from the days of Champlain, who, in 1604, in company with the Sieur de Monts, approached Mount Desert in wonder and entered Frenchman's Bay with profound satisfaction. The Bay still has the original name, just as the island bears to this day a slight modification of the title given it by Champlain—"l'Isle des Monts Desert," the island of the lonely mountains.

Champlain passed on, but other Frenchmen followed him. Nine years later a shipload of emigrants braved the surf that beats on the rocky precipices, guardians of the island, and made a missionary settlement at the entrance to Somes Sound, the estuary to the north of Southwest Harbor that has been called "the one true fiord on the Atlantic Coast of North America from

22

Newfoundland southward.'' The colony—a part of the Acadian settlement—did not survive long, yet Parkman declares that its establishment marked the real beginning of settlements that led to the long conflict between the French and the English in North America.

The next home-makers in the "Isle of Enchantment" came from Massachusetts. Even before 1760 some daring pioneers sought the bold promontories and the inviting valleys of Mount Desert.

Shrewd Francis Bernard, Governor of Massachusetts Bay Colony, decided to do something to claim the Maine country for Massachusetts. He did not see why he might not at the same time win valuable property for himself. At any rate he succeeded in persuading the General Court of Massachusetts to grant to him one half of all Mt. Desert.

Governor Bernard's dreams of an island principality were not to be fulfilled. His estates were confiscated because of his royalist leanings. Later, however, he willed his half of the island to his son John. The General Court confirmed the claim of the son when he proved his loyalty to the Colonies, but he chose to mortgage his possessions for a small sum that he might make his home in England.

In the days following the Revolution Mount Desert real estate was in demand. In 1785 there appeared a claimant for all of the island in the person of Bartolemy de Gregoire, who came from France with his wife. He declared that a grant of the island had been made by Louis XIV to her grandfather, Antoine de la Motte Cadillac, later the founder of Detroit. A letter from Lafayette urged the favorable consideration of the petition. The plea of the Frenchman who had done so

23

much for the Colonies was not to be resisted, and that part of the land then in possession of the state was transferred to the heir.

The "French adventurer" lived for a time at Hull's Cove, then a few miles northwest of the later location of Bar Harbor. Gradually he let his vast estate slip from him. The last sale, made by Henry Jackson for £1247, included twelve islands, which contained in all more than twenty-five hundred acres.

Once Bar Harbor stood for Mount Desert, but the lovers of the wild have entered coves and harbors all around the scores of miles of serrated coast. Now they seek Northeast Harbor and Seal Harbor, Southwest Harbor and Somesville. But why name a few choice resorts when all the island is an alluring treasurehouse of ponds and lakes and craggy mountains; streams and cliffs and mysterious defiles; trees and flowers and luxuriant undergrowth? It is possible to travel twenty miles in one direction and twenty miles in another direction, over this marvelous land of about one hundred square miles, and to discover many surprises in every mile. There is the Sea Wall, a cliff several miles below Southwest Harbor, where the breakers dash in fury. The granite Otter Cliff is approached from the famous ocean drive. Above one of the most delightful of these ocean drives the Cadillac Trail surmounts a sturdy sea cliff.

The Green Mountain Trail looks down on Otter Creek, a little harbor whose limits are fixed by great headlands that are fit company for heights said to be among the greatest between the St. Lawrence and the Amazon. Pemetic Mountain, one of the commanding heights of an island distinguished by the only moun-

GREAT HEAD, GUARDING THE ENTRANCE TO FRENCHMAN'S BAY, MT. DESERT

FRENCHMAN'S BAY, FROM CADILLAC MOUNTAIN. MT. DESERT

tains that approach the Atlantic coast, looks down on a wild, deep gorge and over Eagle Lake to where Bar Harbor seeks the water. Below the Gouldsboro Hills lies Upper Frenchman's Bay, while close to the bay is another gorge, whose deep passage through the rocks provides a way from Bar Harbor to the southern shore of the island.

The lovers of Mount Desert's unparalled scenery long ago determined that it must revert to the people who so prodigally parted with it to the Tory governor and the French adventurer. They wished to see it made a national vacation ground, a sanctuary for the birds that pause here in their migrations, a refuge for the fur-bearing animals that once lived securely in the streams and the ponds. Gradually they gained title to thousands of acres, laid out trails and roads which made practicable trips into the interior and along the coast, while these did not detract from the wild beauty of the surroundings, and finally they prevailed on the United States to take over the lands for the people.

This patriotic gift to the nation became then the nucleus of the Lafayette National Park, which contains great tracts deeds to which were made by the heirs of William Bingham of Philadelphia. And Bingham gained title from the Henry Jackson who bought the last of the holdings of De Gregoire!

CHAPTER III

MOUNT KTAADN, THE HOME OF PAMOLA

WON'T it be good when the tourist can steal on Mount Ktaadn in an automobile?" a thoughtless man said to the lover of the Maine wilderness.

"In an automobile!" was the response. "An automobile road to the most wonderful mountain east of the Rockies, the most resplendent of Maine's hidden glories? It is unthinkable that there should be a turnpike to the skirt of the peaks where, according to Abenakis legend, mysterious Pamola had her awesome residence and held her dread court!

"Let automobiles come within a few miles, if this must be. But it would be folly to talk of doing more than improve the final stretches of the trail so that packhorses could follow them in security. Then we can continue to approach the marvel of the wilderness with reverence; we can be still as successive visions of the Creator's majesty unfold to view; we can rejoice in the knowledge that there is a spot, within easy reach of Boston or New York, where the tumult and the shouting will be forgotten in dreamy hours of communion with tremendous rocky precipices, limpid upland lakes, and lofty sky pastures so recently trodden by the caribou; we can rouse in the night at the sullen roar of the avalanche, and pass the golden mountain days amid the deposits that hide the secrets of the glacial geology of northern Maine."

26

MOUNT KTAADN, THE HOME OF PAMOLA

Modern improvements within the sacred precincts of Ktaadn seem to such enthusiasts as profane as the attempt to call the mountain Katahdin. "Call it Ktaadn," they say, "and so do your best to reproduce in a single syllable the pronunciation of the Indians as they told of their highest land. These savages had such boundless reverence for the mountain that when, in 1804, Charles Turner, the first white man to make the perilous ascent, approached the peak, the native guides refused to climb with him to Pamola's dwelling-place. The angry being, who had the body of a man and the head of a great eagle, would send dire punishment upon them! Every avalanche told of his displeasure, the thunder's roar was the story of his wrath, and the lightnings were only the flashing of his all-seeing eyes."

The Indians have departed, but the glory of Ktaadn remains, hidden in the fastnesses of the lake-girt wilderness, luring the dweller in the haunts of bustle and confusion, promising untold satisfaction to those who are not dismayed by the thought of the days of toil in the canoe and on the trail that are its allies as it maintains its distance from the heedless and the irreverent.

Today many approach the sacred mountain by the West Branch of the Penobscot River, the route chosen long ago by Henry D. Thoreau. But some prefer to vary the route by going from Lily Bay or Moosehead Lake, then by automobile to Kokad-jo or first Roach Pond, then to Ripogenus, entering the West Branch at Ripogenus Gorge, one of the renowned sights of the wilderness. From this the way is down river, past

27

Monument Rock, to the mountain, or still farther down to Abol Falls, and up the Abol trail to the summit.

Some may say that this is nothing but a tiresome list of names. Not to the men or women who have permitted the fever of the wild to have its way in the heart! They are not ashamed to tell how the blood is stirred by the mere tracing of the course to the mountain on a detail map of Maine. How they pity those for whom that map is dumb, lifeless. To them it whispers of the forest trail; it speaks eloquently of the canoe gliding swiftly on the surface of the still reaches of the stream, or poising for a dash through the rapids; it thunders with the waters as they fall from the river into the lake.

After the canoe trip amid the secrets of lakes and falls and rivers comes the trail with its fascinating glimpses of mountain glory, glimpses that finally—if the enshrouding mists are kind—melt into the soul-satisfying view of the monarch whose granite slopes rise 5,268 feet above the sea, without foothills or near mountain neighbors to take away from its solitary grandeur.

The mountain thus disclosed has been described vividly for the author by William F. Dawson, artist-explorer, whose wonderful photographs of Ktaadn plead insistently with those who see them to go into the wilderness and feel the mountain:

"Imagine a giant starfish, the back of which is a nearly level plateau forty-three hundred feet above sea level and more than five hundred acres in extent. The arms to the west and south stretch out radially as great ridges to the plain below, while between are gullies or ravines so steep as to be unclimbable save for the two or three slides. An arm from the southeast corner extends on a great curve first east and then north until it has merely encircled the natural amphitheatre known as the Great or South Basin. That basin is two and one half miles from north to south and one and three quarter miles from east to west. The ridge carries the Main Summit, 5268 feet; the East Peak, 5255 feet; Chimney Peak, about 4700 feet; and Pamola, 4800 feet. Near the Main Peak a minor ridge runs north into the Basin, and the part thus set off constitutes an enormous horseshoe with the opening almost due north. In the middle of the horseshoe is Chimney Pond, 2900 feet in elevation, and surrounded on three sides by granite walls that rise almost perpendicularly for 2000 feet and more.

"From the northern end of the plateau a ridge or elevation extends three or four miles to the north and northeast, finally descending to the plain in gentle slopes. It carries three slight elevations of about 4700 feet total altitude known as the North Peaks. Three miles north of the Main Peak the North Basin extends east for a mile and a half. Its floor is 3700 feet elevation and its width about a mile. Like the South Basin, its plan view is a horseshoe, and its northern walls are so steep that avalanches are of frequent occurrence."

That description was written after a succession of ascents which failed to yield photographs satisfactory to the mountaineer; he had been able to go only in August, when the advancing season makes the trail less difficult. But he resolved to go in early June, that he might surprise the sun in the depths of the great Basin. This trip was made in 1920, after the winter of Maine's greatest snowfall in fifty years. With one companion he pushed on in the face of difficulties that seemed almost unsurmountable, and succeeded in finding the sun ready to make the photograph that accompanies this chapter.

The beginning of what Mr. Dawson has called "a week of romance" was at Staceyville, on the Bangor and Aroostook Railroad. He had chosen the Lunksoos Trail, by way of the East Branch of the Penobscot, in spite of the fact that the river was too deep to ford and the brooks were full. His companion, a seasoned woodsman, thought it possible to make the thirty miles to the mountain, if they would "travel light."

The first night was spent at the Hunt Place of which Thoreau told so long ago. Lunch next day was eaten at the Devil's Elbow, scene of the death of scores of river-drivers who ventured too much in their efforts to break timber jams in Wissataquoik.

Ktaadn Lake is on the Lunksoos Trail. There the party ate their dinner of fish, taken in what is known as one of the unspoiled fishing places of Maine. Sport is good in that region, for there also are bear near the lakes, though not enough of them to satisfy all hunters. The men bound for the mountain were told of two trappers who had gone away disgusted because they had secured only four of the beasts!

From Sandy Stream Pond there is a stiff climb of fourteen hundred feet within three or four miles. The necessity of cutting a trail through fallen trees added to the difficulties of the way, but these merely prepared the men for real enjoyment of their sleep that night on a bed of balsam boughs, under a four pound tent.

At length the climbers started over the mountain, for it was their purpose to descend on the other side

A MORNING VIEW INTO THE SOUTH BASIN, MT. KTAADN, FROM CHIMNEY POND
Photographed and Copyrighted by William F. Dawson

and go on to the West Branch. The first part of the journey, to the Ridge, was made by a route probably never before taken. The only way to pass through the stunted spruce on the plateau beyond the Ridge was along the old caribou trail. This led on toward Abol Slide, which, from the top, looks as if it had no bottom. "Near the top a number of huge bowlders are fastened together, in some indescribable way that bars the path except for an opening near the base known as the Needle's Eye. The smaller rocks are not so well anchored and one must proceed with extreme caution, lowering himself from rock to rock and only occasionally taking a few steps on the steep granite gravel."

The night was spent on a level spot, in a cabin of the Maine Forestry Commission. Next day the arduous climb down the slide was continued until Millinocket Tote Road greeted the men of the trail, and led them on to the West Branch. There they took to the water and marvelled that "no modern machinery functions more beautifully than the children of the forest when handling a canoe."

Ambejijis Lake and Pemadumcook Lake were waiting for the pilgrims of 1920, as for Thoreau in 1846. But a little later they entered the train that would have been disdained by the earlier visitor. And next day the photographer was back in the city, while his guide was making ready for more of the visitors who have learned to hearken to the call of the Maine Wilderness.

CHAPTER IV

THROUGH MAINE IN A CANOE

IT is not strange that Massachusetts tried her best to hold fast to Maine. For nearly fifty years she resented the proposed separation of her possession to the north from the day, in 1775, when Governor Bowdoin spoke of the design of these countries to set up a separate government as "of very evil tendency."

Opposition might have been even more spirited if anyone had foreseen the day when the demand for lumber would make invaluable the stores of timber so vast that, even after years of wasteful cutting, there still remain thousands of square miles of dense woodland. No one dreamed of the harnessing of water power like that, for instance, at Lewiston, where there are thirteen thousand horse power, and this is but one of the vast developments, actual and possible, in a state where there is said to be more undeveloped water power than in any other section of the eastern part of the country.

The commercial and economic possibilities of Maine are great, but in the mind of many they are overshadowed by the thought that this is the country for the sportsman. To these the great trees of the endless forests that rise like needles toward the sky speak, not of lumber, but of the camp, and the moose, and the trail, and the matchless music made by the wind as it sighs through the branches. The lakes and the rivers

SUPPER ON ROCKY POND, MAINE

SURPRISING THE DEER BY FLASHLIGHT

say nothing of commerce; their message is for the fisherman and the master of the fragile canoe.

An editorial writer in the New York *Times* once said, "No man in Maine can walk abroad in his sleep without risking a fall into lake water." And it is almost as difficult to avoid catching fish in these lakes. They say that some anglers at Rangeley Lakes refuse to take home trout under three pounds in weight; they throw them back that the fish may have time to grow up! Yet it must not be thought that the fish are caught so easily that there is no sport in their conquest.

The woods are full of deer, and the moose await the coming of those who seek them with camera: there is no open season for these monarchs of the forest, though the hunter is permitted to kill two deer in the brief season. There is no close season on bears or bobcats; in fact that is a state bounty to those who bring in their pelts.

But the great sport in Maine is canoeing. A map of the possible canoe routes in the state looks like the astronomer's chart of the canals on Mars. Some of them, isolated, are in the southwest section of the state, but most of them are in the wilderness country farther north. There they connect and interlock so completely that it is possible to travel close to a thousand miles in this alluring fashion, usually, in the season, within easy reach of camps and guides and assistance in transporting supplies and canoes over the larger carries.

One, of the milder canoeing ventures may be made on the Kennebec, both below and above Augusta, the old Koussinoc of the Abenakis. A second canoeing ground is Lake Sebago, which Portland claims as her own particular lake. Its picturesque rock-bound shores, where trees find precarious foothold, are as attractive for the tourist who wishes to feast his eyes on the glories about him, as are the fish in the deep waters for those who prefer to think of a feast later by the camp fire.

A vacation experience for the more ambitious is offered by the Rangeley Lake chain, which includes Lake Umbagog in New Hampshire. Once a visitor declared, "Who has not seen Rangeley is disqualified for speaking on New England's scenic beauty." Then he went on to tell how it appealed to every sense: "to the sight, with crystal waters and spire-like pines, covering strange, half-penetrable shadows; to the hearing, with those sounds which only the trained woodsmen can interpret; to the smell, with odors replete with associations; and to the touch, with the cool cleanliness of the forests and breezes that are only the undertone of the great, free woods that never sleep, but are forever rocking the tops of the loftiest trees and drawing the scudding clouds across the mountain peaks."

The sportsman who has fished and canoed on Rangeley will have abundant appetite for the yet greater fascination of the more northerly canoe routes. Of these that down the Allagash River is by many held to be the most wonderful trip of its kind on the continent. Two hundred and three miles of river and lake, of falls and rapids, of carries through the forest, of camps amid the silent solitude of the Maine woods! Women as well as men make the journey, which requires at least eight days, though it is far better to take four weeks and give opportunity for wilderness joy to soak in so that it will never come out.

The starting point is on Moosehead Lake, which

34

POLING UP MILNOCKET STREAM

LOOKING UP MOOSE RIVER TO BRASSUA LAKE FROM MT. KINEO

Thoreau called "a suitably wild-looking sheet of water, sprinkled with small, low islands, covered with shaggy spruce and other wildwood." Years have passed, but the general aspect of the country is much as it was when Thoreau paddled over its waters. Mount Kineo still frowns down on the lake, which is of princely size —twelve miles wide and thirty miles long.

The West Branch of the Penobscot approaches within a few miles of Moosehead. Northeast Carry is the attractive name given to the portage that opens the way to twenty miles of delightful river journeying. And this is only the beginning. Chesuncook Lake leads to Umbazooksus Stream, and Umbazooksus Lake. Carries varying from ten rods to a mile are the links that unite the lake and river. When Allagash River is entered, the journey is interrupted only by the Falls until the St. John River is reached at Fort Kent. But even then attractions do not cease. Across the stream in New Brunswick live descendants of the Acadians, and twelve miles down the St. John are the Grand Falls, where water power waits for complete development that will give astonishing results. On the American side is Aroostook County, the famous potato-raising region where a farmer has succeeded in growing 2672 bushels in a five-acre plot.

The St. John River itself offers a canoe trip even longer than the Allagash, a trip full of thrills and surprises for more than two hundred miles. Then, for variety, there is the journey up the West Branch of the Penobscot, and that on the East Branch, and numerous side trips among the lakes and rivers which have names as strange and scenery as inviting as those on the longer routes.

CHAPTER V

SAUNTERING THROUGH NEW HAMPSHIRE

TO many people New Hampshire means the White Mountains, and Lake Winnepesaukee; and it does not occur to them that it is worth their while to know anything about parts of the state not included in the wonderful mountain section, except as they are compelled to cross a few counties more or less on the way to the lake whose name twists in accordance with the contour of its shore line, or to the mountains that pierce the clouds to the north of the lake.

Yet New Hampshire has much to offer the visitor who is willing to be leisurely, who is ready to saunter along the roads that are so wonderfully fine for the automobile. But think of the other roads on which the driver of an automobile would not dream of going! Think also of the tracks and paths, as well as of the woodlands by the roadside!

Portsmouth is a fine starting point either for the automobilist or for the walker. But even here the walker has the advantage, for he can seek out picturesque corners that are hidden from the tourist who travels more prosaically. He will find lanes bordered by nameless old houses, with doorways and porticoes over which the architect would rave, as well as splendid trees that lean affectionately toward their neighbors or guard the gateways to gardens that speak of past generations. He will find churches whose architecture would loudly proclaim

36

their New England origin even if they could be transported a thousand miles away. He will pause before the historic Warner house, with its stately row of five dormer windows facing the street, and the curious octagon lantern on the roof, or will wander into the spacious grounds of the rambling, many-gabled Wentworth house that is eloquent with the legend of the fair Amy who became the wife of Governor Banning Wentworth, to the surprise of all her friends as well as his own, thus giving the Quaker Poet the theme for the ballad that ends—

> " Oh, rank is good, and gold is fair,
> And high and low mate ill;
> But love has never known a law
> Beyond its own sweet will."

Let the first walk from Portsmouth be in the direction of Exeter, home of Phillips Exeter Academy, enshrined in the affections of many because of the great men who—like George Bancroft—passed from its doors to win fame for themselves and be a blessing to the country.

There is a roundabout automobile road from Exeter, through bustling Manchester, to the region of Amherst, birthplace of Horace Greeley, serene in its setting among the hills. But it is so much better to disregard roads and take a route through Danville and Derry to Litchfield, where the brooks that play among the trees contest with the village the right to first attention.

From Litchfield the road is short to Milford, on the Souhegan River, tributary of the Merrimac. The stone bridge, the tumbling waters, the square with its interlacing trees, the hills around about, and the roads that

37

rise and fall like the billows of the sea, make such an appealing series of pictures that it is a temptation to feel that the Granite State can offer nothing finer than this section of the southern hill country.

Mistake! Go on, still " across lots," to Mount Monadnock, the lonely sentinel mountain, visible from seven states, famous landmark of the Indians, celebrated alike by poets and essayists and artists. Nathaniel Hawthorne spoke of it as "a sapphire cloud against the sky."

A few miles from Monadnock are the Swanzeys, among their ponds, all famous because one of them, West Swanzey, was the original village of Denman Thompson's Old Homestead.

At West Swanzey, on the Ashland River, the man of leisure finds a series of rambles along the streams and ponds, with bits of country between, that will lead at length to the Contoocook River.

Down below the point of union of the Contoocook and the Merrimac, Concord proudly guards the banks of the stream, its cosy streets and its inviting homes the fit setting for the old state house.

From Concord there is no better way to approach the famous lakes of central New Hampshire than along the Merrimac. For those who must use a road, there is a good highway along the river to Franklin, then close to the outlet of Winnisquam Lake that enters the stream at this point. But for those who have learned the keen delight of "stream following," the road has no attractions.

Winnisquam Lake, where the loon sends out its weird call and the fish bite with pleasant freedom, is the portal to the still greater glories of Winnepesaukee,

38

AIR VIEW OF CONCORD, NEW HAMPSHIRE, SHOWING CAPITOL AND MERRIMAC RIVER
Photo by the Kimball Studios, Concord

queen of New Hampshire lakes, which the Indians called "The Smile of the Great Spirit." Like a great octopus it spreads its tentacles out into the surrounding country. Intricate shore lines; broad reaches where the motor boat pounds freely along for miles; narrow channels where the shores crowd close together; islands wooded, rocky, mysterious; bays that lead to green slopes where farm lands cluster around a village clothed in white; and beaches, where bathers throng; jutting headlands where the wind moans among the branches of the pines; retired nooks where the sportsman drifts in his dory, almost too lazy to draw in the fish that would rouse him to action.

One of the greatest charms of Lake Winnepesaukee —or Winipissioket Pond, as it was called on an early map—is the distant view of peaks of the White Mountains. Forest-covered Ossippee and Red Hill, the peaks of the Sandwich Range, and Belknap are visible from various points. Mount Chocorua shows up at a distance from Three Mile Island, where the Appalachian Mountaineers have a club-house. Members gathered there about the camp fire have discussed the fascinating story of the naming of the mountain to the north, which cannot be told without speaking of Passaconaway, Wonnalancet and Kankamagus. These Indians and their associates wandered here and there among the valleys and the lakes and climbed the slopes of the mountains that cluster in such splendid array for sixty miles and more north of Winnepesaukee and almost entirely across the narrowing width of New Hampshire between the Connecticut River and the slopes that look off toward the Saco and beautiful Upper Kezar Pond, just over the boundary line of Maine.

A map of 1776 called the Saco the Pigwakket. The same name was given to the mountain now called Chocorua, in memory of a powerful chieftain who lived near its base.

With a modesty that is difficult to understand, the early settlers called the mountains as a whole the "White Hills." Evidently they did not realize that many of them range in height from four thousand to six thousand feet or even more. The Indians were less prosaic; their name was "The Mountains with Snowy Foreheads."

The White Mountain region has as many opportunities for rambling as it has mountains. For the visitor who enters by way of Lake Winnepesaukee, there is no better route into the heart of the mysteries than from Melvin Village northeast to Chatham, past peaks whose rugged beauty is so great that it seems a wonder they are not better known, along the shores of ponds that might as well be called lakes, through valleys and by winding water courses, into the heart of the White Mountain National Forest, where roads and trails and camping sites are provided in profusion, as marked plainly on the map of the forest, which should be the companion of every visitor to the region.

Far over toward the twists and turns in the Connecticut River, Mount Starr King rises above the headwaters of Moose River, a western tributary of the Androscoggin, while to the south of the stream is a group of a dozen peaks that dominate half a dozen ridges, separated by wild ravines. Some of these mountains—Mount Madison and Mount Adams among them—are only a few hundred feet behind Mount Washington, the king of them all.

LOST RIVER, ISSUING FROM UNDERGROUND CAVERN, WHITE MOUNTAINS

HAYING SEASON IN THE WHITE MOUNTAINS
View from Bethlehem, New Hampshire

VIEW FROM CARRIAGE ROAD, ACROSS GREAT GULF
Mt. Washington, after the Great Storm of September 30, 1915

To the southwest of Mount Adams is the Castellated Ridge, famous because of the scene of wild beauty glimpsed from its various vantage points. Far below, in the Ravine of the Castles, Castle Brook descends madly amid the rocks buried in the depths of the forest, seeking Israel's River, on the way to the Connecticut.

Before Mount Washington itself is approached, it is well to saunter in from the west, beginning perhaps at Bethlehem, where the vale is of surpassing loveliness, going over to Franconia and—where the mountains come so close together—Franconia Notch, with its Old Man of the Mountain and the Flume, where rocky walls, nine hundred feet long and seventy feet deep, shut out the sun except at mid-day.

To the east of Franconia Notch is Bretton Woods, the name of which is a reminder of old England. In 1772 Governor Wentworth granted the land in this section to his cousin, whose home was at Bretton Hill in Yorkshire. The picturesque name might have been lost forever, for in 1832 it was changed to Carrol. But in 1902 some wise delver in historic lore discovered the earlier name and its significance, and succeeded in having it restored.

Another historic name is that given to Crawford Notch, to the south of Bretton Woods. Ethan Allan Crawford was not only the proprietor of the first hotel in this region, but he was the maker of the first footpath to Mount Washington, and the first shelter on the summit of the mountain.

Crawford's Notch—one of the outstanding glories of the White Mountains, and the source of the Saco River—was discovered by Timothy Nash, pioneer, who had sought the wilderness to make a home for his family. One day, while in pursuit of a moose, he found himself in the dark depths of the Notch. Later he told of his discovery to Governor Wentworth, who promised him a grant of land if he would lead a horse through the Notch. The problem was to get a horse into the pass; progress would be comparatively easy after that had been done. With the help of a companion, ingenious as himself, he hoisted a horse by ropes over the rocks into the Notch. And he had his reward, for here, in 1773, the governor gave 184 acres to the two men. A month later they sold the ground for ninety pounds, but it is still known as Nash and Sawyer's Location, and it is so marked in the map of the New Hampshire State Forest Reservation, within the White Mountain National Forest, which includes the Notch.

All these features of the White Mountain region, wonderful as they are, are but preparatory to the greatest feature of all, Mount Washington, which, from its height of 6,293 feet, looks royally down on the twenty-three peaks whose elevation exceeds four thousand feet, as well as on countless ridges and mountains that would, in many other locations in the East, be spoken of as respectable eminences.

Mount Washington is so easy of access that appreciation of its wonders need not be reserved for the few. For those who like a real scramble, there is a practicable route up Tuckerman Ravine. The fact that this requires a climb of one thousand feet up a wall where the grade approaches fifty per cent and that provision must be made for cutting steps in the ice and for roping climbers together, adds to the desirability of the trip. There are also reasonably good approaches over the northern peak of the Presidential Range, or

42

from the direction of the peaks to the south, while, for those who seek greater ease, there are the carriage road and the cog railway.

Visitors to the mountain have learned to beware of the sudden descent of autumn storms, which usually focus about the tiny mountain tarns on the south slope, known as the Lakes of the Clouds. William Francis Dawson, one of the most venturesome spirits in the Appalachian Club, encountered one of these storms on September 24, 1915, and narrowly escaped to tell the tale. His start was made from Crawfords. First he went through the forest on Mount Clinton, then proceeded along six miles of the heights toward the goal. "That sky line promenade, with nothing to obstruct the view but Washington itself," Mr. Dawson afterward wrote to the author of this volume, "is one of the finest in New England, and that day there was neither cloud nor haze. Mount Pleasant and Mount Franklin were passed, and then the path skirted the precipitous head wall of Oakes Gulf."

Fortunately the climber met two descending tourists, who, telling him he would find no food at the Appalachian Mountain Club hut at the Lakes of the Clouds, and that the Summit House had just closed for the season, gave him some of their lunch.

In company with the keeper of the hut, and five others, he went to sleep after a beautiful sunset. But the weather changed during the night, and for five days the little company was stormbound. Food was eaten sparingly, for there was little beside the lunch received from the descending tourists. The wind blew with a velocity unknown before in forty years. Thousands

43

of trees were blown down on the lower slopes of the mountain.

From Saturday until Thursday the storm continued. Then the sun rose clear and disclosed what Mr. Dawson said was the most beautiful sight he had ever seen. "The upper four hundred feet of Mount Monroe rose before us, all white with frost, save where the sun touched the high spots with rose. The storm was over, the wind had gone down, and not a cloud remained above us, but a thousand feet below was an ocean of clouds, and here and there the higher peaks showed above like islands in the ocean. Everything above 4000 feet was white with frost. On the hut chimney was a distinct feather's plume, two feet long. As we ascended the cone to the summit the frost formations kept increasing in size until, at the very top, some of them were fully five feet in length. Every stick and stone was so cold during the storm that it had collected the moisture from the fog in the form of beautiful frost feathers."

Mr. Dawson succeeded in taking some wonderful pictures of these frost formations. They are his souvenirs of one of the narrowest escapes climbers on Mount Washington ever had.

CHAPTER VI

ON "THE LONG TRAIL" IN VERMONT

THOSE who become enthusiastic when they talk of the surpassing scenery of Vermont are in good company. There is a record that in 1790 George Washington, just after entering the southwest corner of Vermont, when on his notable horseback journey which had for its object the discussion of the possibility of Vermont's entrance to the Federal Union, stood enraptured when on the road to Pownal Center.

That journey of Washington marked the end of a generation of disputes between New Hampshire and New York for the country west of the Connecticut. Governor Banning Wentworth of New Hampshire created one hundred and thirty-eight "New Hampshire Grants" west of the river, in spite of New York's claim to jurisdiction. The rights of the settlers of the Grants were defended by the Green Mountain Boys, of whom Ethan Allen was the leader.

The first of the Grants was Bennington, the city on the Walloomsac, a few miles north of the Pownal Intervale which charmed Washington in 1790, noted for the beauty of the view from the top of the Battle Monument.

The hill of the Bennington Battle Monument, like the mountains that surround Bennington, really belongs to the Taconics, though all are popularly thought of as a part of the Green Mountain chain that stretches from the Massachusetts line, where this is crossed by the

Deerfield River, and on for one hundred and fifty-eight miles to the Canadian border.

Determined to persuade others of what they felt to be the preëminence of the Green Mountains, either for a summer's sojourn or a walking or motor trip of a few days or weeks, the members of the Green Mountain Club in 1910 began to blaze The Long Trail along the mountains from the Massachusetts line to the Canadian border. By enlisting the aid of residents near the route and of the State Forest Service they have succeeded in providing a practicable route almost all the way, and the few gaps will be filled before long. Side trails also have been equipped, so that access is easy to the crowning glories of a state that has been called by many travelers the most beautiful territory of its size in the United States.

One of the services performed by the Green Mountain Club is the preparation of leaflets and booklets describing the Long Trail in whole or in part, and telling of trips that have been taken over its rugged miles. Of particular value is a leaflet outlining a "Ten Days' Tramp on the Long Trail," with sensible hints for the tramper. Some of these documents may be secured from the Secretary of the Club at Burlington. These should be supplemented by the Road Map of Vermont and companion booklets issued by the Secretary of State, Publicity Department, Montpelier.

Thus provided, the traveler is ready for the joy-giving, mind-invigorating, health-preserving, soul-satisfying plunge into the Green Mountains at any one of a score of points, or for the wondrous pilgrimage through "the only state east of the Rockies traversed from end to end by a mountain range."

46

IN A MARBLE QUARRY, RUTLAND, VERMONT

GATHERING MAPLE SAP IN VERMONT

ON "THE LONG TRAIL" IN VERMONT

It is startling to learn that in the comparatively small area of the state there are 494 peaks with an elevation of 2000 feet or higher, while 89 are 3000 feet or over, and four are 4000 feet. 459 of these lofty peaks are in the southern half of the state.

If The Long Trail is approached from Bennington, the climber will find himself at once among a bewildering array of eminences that look down on so many towns in Vermont and Massachusetts that it is difficult to keep track of them; it is said that fifty towns can be counted from Newfane Hill in Windham county. From Stratton Mountain, to the east of the Trail, portions of four states may be seen.

Green Mountain at Manchester is like a vast sea billow reaching gently down to the valley, while Mount Aeolus, farther north, raises its tree-clad slopes high above the winding brooks that pick their way daintily through the meadows at its base. One of the temptations to side trips will come when the Trail leads close to the headwaters of the Ottagueechee River. The stream as it winds amid the green meadows at Sherburne with graceful ridges rising on either side and the shadow of clouds and trees reflected in its cool depths, speaks with a luring voice.

Back to the Trail, and up to Killington Peak, 4241 feet high, the second highest peak in Vermont, which lords it over half a dozen mountains, each more than three thousand feet high, all of these rising from the same base as Killington. Here the Trail climber feels himself at the heart of Vermont's wilderness. The ascent is sometimes difficult, but the view from the summit is sublime. The eye sweeps from Lake

47

Champlain and Lake George, with the Adirondacks beyond, to the White Mountains.

Then comes twin-peaked Bread Loaf Mountain, with its outlook that takes in the four highest peaks of the State, and tributary glens and lakes. The automobile road part-way up the mountain is one of the finest drives in the State.

By this time the follower of the Trail will probably have exhausted his adjectives and will look out in silence when he stands on the summit of Lincoln, 4024 feet high, over the forested slopes that rise and fall to south, to west, to north, to east, and when he comes to Camel's Hump he will wonder how he could have thought that earlier views could not be surpassed. For he will find that other mountains have withdrawn to a distance, so that, as he stands on bare rock, above the timber line, he beholds wide stretches of lower lands. Behind him on one side there is a precipice four hundred feet higher that gives a taste of real Rocky Mountain scenery. Away to the south reaches the ridge over which the climber has come.

Twenty miles to the north, Mount Mansfield towers above all its fellows, to a height of 4457 feet. On the eastern side of this mountain are the Rock of Terror and the Cave of the Winds, and far below are the depths and bordering cliffs of Smuggler's Notch.

Between Mount Mansfield and the Canadian border there are many outstanding peaks, but the greatest of them all is Jay Peak, from whose summit the tourist may, when weather conditions are favorable, descry the Montreal and Ottawa Valleys, the mountains beyond the St. Lawrence, the mountains and the headwaters of the Connecticut River, the Chaudiere and Androscoggin

48

THE CAMEL'S HUMP, GREEN MOUNTAINS, VERMONT

MOHAWK VALLEY, VERMONT, LOOKING EAST INTO NEW HAMPSHIRE
Showing Connecticut River Covered Bridge, Dixville Mountains in Distance

Valleys, the Presidential Range of the White Mountains, the northern Green Mountain peaks, nearly the entire length of Lake Champlain, with the Andirondacks beyond, the Richelieu River from the point where it receives the waters of Lake Champlain until it empties into the St. Lawrence, as well as Lake Willoughby, with its guardians Mount Pisgah and Mount Hor, and that other lake whose name speaks so enticingly of the Indians who delighted to paddle on its glassy surface—Memphremagog.

Lake Memphremagog is the capital feature of the remarkable lake region of Northeastern Vermont, where there are nearly two hundred lakes and ponds.

Of the thirty-two miles of Memphremagog between Newport, Vermont, and Magog, Canada, but one-fifth is in Vermont. This international lake is overlooked by towering summits in both countries, among them Owl's Head and Orford. Orford is the highest peak in eastern Canada, while Owl's Head has been famous for two generations as the annual meeting place of a lodge of Masons. On June 24 the favored members of the secret order seek a part of a cleft near the summit—a natural lodge room of adequate size, bounded by rocky walls that rise precipitously twenty feet high. Thus, when the Masons enter their hall in the mountain, they are hidden in the cleft of the rock. And when the session is adjourned, they mount to the summit vantage ground where they can look away one hundred miles to Montreal, the city by the St. Lawrence.

CHAPTER VII

BOSTON, THE CITY OF THE GOLDEN DOME

IT is recorded that before Phillips Brooks would take Dean Stanley on a tour of his native Boston, he first led him to the cupola above the dome of the State House that he might revel in the panorama of Boston old and new laid out at his feet. It is still better to supplement such a pilgrimage to the State House by a trip to the roof of one of the business buildings looking down on the Common. The only disadvantage in looking out on the city from such a point of vantage is that the dome of the House of the Sacred Codfish hides certain landmarks toward Charlestown. But this deprivation is atoned for by having as a part of the picture the State House itself.

Even more important than the State House as a central feature of old Boston is the Common—resort of the populace from the days of the Puritans, playground of boys and girls of nearly three centuries, favorite pasture of the gentle Boston cow for more than half that time. The fifty acres that slope gently down Beacon Hill from the State House to Boylston and Tremont Streets have been jealously guarded from all intrusion.

The northern boundary of Boston Common is Beacon Street, for many years bordered by the homes of notables, chief of these being John Hancock. Over the hill is the beautiful Charles River.

Today the broad estuary of the Charles, to the

FANEUIL HALL, BOSTON
Erected 1742

KING'S CHAPEL, BOSTON
Erected 1753

"ELMWOOD," JAMES RUSSELL LOWELL'S HOUSE, CAMBRIDGE, MASSACHUSETTS

northwest of the observer on the roof of the building by the Common, is more attractive than it was in the days of the author of the Declaration of Independence. At a distance is the Harvard Bridge. Beyond it, in Cambridge, are the white walls of the famous Massachusetts Institute of Technology. Still farther away, but out of sight, are the buildings of Harvard University, whose students show their good taste by rowing on the inimitable Charles, or by looking at the twinkling lights that reach up the hill toward the State House across a region that once was a favorite dwelling place of the great, though now it is largely given over to the dwellers from foreign lands who, if they look to the north, can see Old North Church, from whose steeple the signal lanterns were hung for Paul Revere. Over the Charles in Charlestown rises Bunker Hill Monument, the shaft that has been a.1 inspiration to millions of liberty-loving men and women.

Within a few squares on the east and northeast are easily discerned the Old South Church, the old State House from whose balcony the Declaration of Independence was proclaimed, King's Chapel, the worshiping place of loyalists during the Revolution, and Faneuil Hall, "the Cradle of American Liberty." Beyond these is the great Custom House tower, the most conspicuous landmark in the city, rising high above a Greek columned structure that would be memorable even without the tower.

Almost at the base of the building that affords the bird's-eye view of Boston is "Brimstone Corner," where stands Park Street Congregational Church, with its wonderfully graceful steeple that speaks of Sir Christopher Wren, and, under its shadow, the Granary

Burying Ground, in which famous men of Revolutionary days lie serenely within a stone's throw of that other graveyard about King's Chapel where are buried some of those with whom, when living, they were not always on speaking terms.

Without a guide it is difficult for a stranger to pass quickly among the relics of the Revolution that cluster so thickly to the east of the Common. A Bostonian, if he is thoroughly honest, would probably be willing to say that it is not always easy for him to give another directions for finding his way, or even to find his own way, through the maze of streets that have been said to follow the windings of old cow paths.

The distant view of the water front whets the appetite for a stroll along the wharves and among the shipping. The famous T Wharf, close to the Custom House, is a good starting point. After the tour is completed is a good time to take a boat and cruise among the numerous islands of the strangely picturesque harbor.

An excursion that should be taken by all means is to Revere Beach. There is afforded a typical study of what the city is doing to give relaxation to its residents. Since 1892 the municipality has built up a series of parks extraordinary. These range in size from the Charlesbank Playground of ten acres to reservations like that of the Blue Hills south of town. Today the Metropolitan Park District controls nearly ten thousand acres of playground in the hills, in the valleys and along the rivers for twenty miles around.

The fathers who laid out Tremont Street would surely have been surprised if they could have known that some day this street would point toward one of these pleasure grounds. At first the streets was named Trimount because it looked toward three peaks of the Blue Hills. From Trimount the ascent—or was it a descent?—to Tremont was easy.

These Blue Hills may be seen from the chosen eyrie of the sightseer, at the edge of the Common. And from them the eye may sweep to the southwest, over toward Roxbury, the town of early days which was "well watered with cool and pleasant springs issuing forth from the rocky hills, and with small freshets watering the valley of the fertile town."

To the north of the old region of springs, but to the west of the Common are some of the modern city's most famous buildings. Here is the Back Bay territory, whose towers and spires rise in pleasing profusion and variety. The New Old South Church is there, with colonial tombstones set in its walls. Trinity Church also is there, and by its side is the St. Gaudens statue of Phillips Brooks, its most famous rector. The Boston Public Library is a near neighbor, with its St. Gaudens lions, the Abbey pictures of the Holy Grail, the Sargent decorations, and the section of the prisoners' dock where, in Boston, England, in 1607, the Pilgrims Bradford and Brewster were tried.

And when, at length, all the landmarks, seen first from the height, have been examined in detail on the ground, it is wise to climb once more to the State House Cupola—or, better still, to a building from which the State House can be seen—for the last lingering glimpses of the City of the Golden Dome.

CHAPTER VIII

ON THE ROAD OUT OF BOSTON

BOSTON'S Metropolitan Park System reaches out to the north so as to include a portion of the Middlesex Fells, the famous tract of woodland in a region of low hills. The Medford and Andover turnpike skirts the Fells which are bounded roughly by Stoneham, Woburn, Winchester, Medford, Malden, and Melrose.

Beyond Andover the road approaches the Merrimac River opposite Haverhill, whose citizens rejoice in the possession of Fernside Farm, the birthplace of John G. Whittier. When he was born in 1807 the house was one hundred and fifteen years old, and it looks as if it were still good for a few hundred years.

From Haverhill the turnpike follows the Merrimac down to the sea at Newburyport, the old seaside town so full of reminders of a sturdy past, prominent among them being the Old South Church. This was built in 1750, but it stands almost exactly as it was in the beginning. From its pulpit George Whitefield thundered fiery invectives and made stirring appeals, and in the crypt he was buried.

From Newburyport the road turns back toward Boston, passing through the country of the Plum Island Marshes, part of the salt meadows which stretch from Cape Ann to Rye, New Hampshire. These curious lands—of which there are about one hundred and sixty square miles in all—have been formed by the gathering

INTERIOR OF OLD SOUTH CHURCH, NEWBURYPORT, MASSACHUSETTS
Erected 1750

NATHANIEL HAWTHORNE'S "WAYSIDE," CONCORD, MASSACHUSETTS

THE HOUSE OF SEVEN GABLES, SALEM, MASSACHUSETTS

of sediment from the river in basins bounded by the mainland and the heaped-up sand beaches. Gradually the land has been built up until it is comparatively dry except at high tide. Portions of these marshes have been drained by means of dikes and have been found very fertile.

Down where its marshes reach to the sea, Gloucester Harbor marks the extreme northern end of Massachusetts Bay. Within this harbor the Puritans first found shelter and made the land when they came to the New England coast. The old town abounds in picturesque nooks and corners.

Near neighbor to Gloucester is Salem, once a port of world-wide fame. For more than one hundred years ships carried its name to the seven seas. It is recorded that in 1807 one hundred and fifty-five deep commerce carriers were owned there, and that the first merchant vessel to sail around the world was the *Minerva,* commanded by a Salem man for a Salem owner.

In the Peabody Museum are treasured many things that speak of those heroic days—as well as of days less heroic when the witch delusion was still in the land. Yet most people prefer to spend their time in the open, going to Gallows Hill, where nineteen people were executed for witchcraft in 1692, to the House of Seven Gables, where Hawthorne wrote The Scarlet Letter, to the Endicott Pear Tree at Danversport, planted by John Endicott in 1632, or to the Needham Homestead in West Peabody, two hundred and fifty years old and occupied by the tenth generation in descent from the builder.

Almost at every turn in the Massachusetts Bay country are houses that were built in the days of

Anthony Needham, of Youlgrave, England, the first
owner of the Needham house. Over at Saugus Broadhearth is more than twenty years older. It was built
the year after the opening of "ye Iron Works" opposite,
the first iron foundry in America.

Broadhearth, which is now in the possession of the
Wallace Nutting Corporation, has a picturesque over-
hang, as has also the neighboring Bennet-Boardman
house, where the Society for the Preservation of New
England Antiquities has done effective work in making
the property available for those who wish to inspect it.

Saugus is on the crooked Saugus River, another
of the short but beautiful streams of northeastern
Massachusetts, with Lynn at the mouth, named in honor
of Rev. Samuel Whiting of King's Lin, England, his
former home.

The distance required for the circular tour that
ends soon after Lynn is left behind is not great, but
the interest of the country and the towns passed through
is so great that it is difficult to complete it in a single
day. But a trip that may well be made in a day is out
to Lexington and Concord and up the Concord River
to Lowell on the Merrimac.

The pilgrim to Lexington should pause at the
Common, study the battleground where the patriots
resisted aggression on that April day in 1775, and look
in at the Clarke House, in which John Hancock and
Samuel Adams were resting when Paul Revere warned
them of danger.

Over at Concord he would of course see, in addition
to the battlefield and the monument of the Minute Men,
Hawthorne's Old Manse, as well as the Emerson and
Alcott houses. Those who gave the town its name

56

might have chosen differently if they could have read the future. But they were merely reading the past. When they bought the land, Musketaquid, from the Indians they thought Concord was the only possible name, because everything was so harmonious.

The Concord enters the Merrimac where Lowell takes power from the latter stream, which has been called the most useful river of its size in America, because of the water power developments at Lowell, as well as farther up and down the river.

There is a river nearer Boston that is famous not for water power, but for beauty. From the broad stretch close to the State House to its source thirty miles away the Charles winds amid surroundings of utmost charm. That is, the direct distance from source to mouth is only thirty miles, but those who follow the windings of the river will have to travel sixty-seven miles. They will see the section on which Longfellow delighted to look from his window and the Hemlock Gorge that has been made a part of the Metropolitan Park System. They will go to Watertown, where, on the river bank, is the home of the Perkins Institution for the Blind, whose English Gothic buildings cluster about a central tower that has been called a poem in stone—even if it is made of cement!

Up stream from Watertown Waltham looks out on Prospect Hill, four hundred and sixty feet above the village, which, from its summit, offers a view of the windings of the river that should be complemented by the view from Doublet Hill, three miles farther south.

Within reach of the Charles are the buildings of Wellesley College, on a campus as attractive as the character of Miss Freeman, long president of the

57

institution, whose life-ideals were expressed to one who urged her to write books instead of using all her strength in interviews with her girls. She replied:

"I am trying to make girls happier and wiser. Books don't help much toward that. They are entertaining enough, but really dead things. Why should I make more of them? It is people that count. You want to put yourself into people; they touch other people; these, others still, and so you go on working forever."

Another as earnest as the teacher whom Wellesley delights to honor went more than two hundred years earlier to Natick. His name was John Eliot. On the banks of the Charles he gathered his Indian friends about him after his settlement there in 1650, persevering in his efforts on their behalf until many of them were splendid specimens of Christian manhood. The town was incorporated in 1679, and for seven years all the officers were Indians.

The people of Natick, in common with the students from Wellesley, frequently resort to the top of Pegan Hill, several miles away, for a restful view of the windings of the Charles. On a cloudy day they can see also the waters of the Atlantic. Sometimes, however, they prefer to walk north to Lake Cochituate, where seekers after quiet beauty have learned that it is worth while to go at all seasons.

The lake reaches north almost to South Sudbury, on the road to Worcester, the location of Longfellow's Wayside Inn, where both Washington and Lafayette were guests. When they were in the village they must have admired the two old oaks before the Wayside Inn whose branches shade a stretch of ground two hundred feet long.

There are twenty miles more of rural beauty on the road from the Sudbury River to Worcester, the city which boasts of being "the first town in the United States to buy lands with public funds for park purposes." Elm Park includes the historic purchase, which was the nucleus of the 1065 acres now open to the public. The Old Common also belongs to the park system. Here was the training ground of the Minute Men before and during the Revolution. Quinsigamond Pond, one of the largest bodies of water in the State, is the gem of the city's pleasure grounds with its miles of drives along the wooded, indented shore.

At Westboro, twelve miles southeast, Eli Whitney was born, while Elias Howe was born at Spencer, a few miles west. Clara Barton, founder of the Red Cross, first saw the light at Bartlett's Upper Mill, almost directly south. Later she lived on a farm on the banks of French River, taught school for sixteen years at North Oxford and elsewhere in the neighborhood. Then, after half a century of Red Cross service, she was buried at North Oxford, where the road from Winchester touches French River.

Let those who stand on the hallowed spot recall the fact that, two nights before her death, she roused from sleep and whispered:

"I dreamed I was back in battle....Once again I stood by the soldiers....I crept around once more, trying to give them at least a drink of water to cool their parched lips....Then I woke to hear myself groan....I am ashamed that I murmur."

CHAPTER IX

FROM BOSTON TO CAPE COD

AS the crow flies the distance from Boston to Cape Cod is only about fifty miles. In an airship the trip could be made in little more than half an hour. But it is far better to take the rambling route along the shores of Massachusetts Bay and Cape Cod Bay. Between Plymouth and the Cape Cod Canal there is an eighteen-mile gap in the railroad, and it becomes necessary for the traveler to choose a roundabout inland route—that is, unless he is following the coast by automobile, or is ready to cover the gap on foot. With a congenial companion a delightful week might be spent in a walking trip between Boston and the sandy point where the Pilgrims landed. What could be better than to follow from one end to the other the Old Coast Road of the Pilgrims, the oldest main road in New England, going thus in the steps of Myles Standish who traveled many times between Plymouth and Boston on errands for the little colony on Cape Cod Bay?

Go along the highway, turning aside into by-paths whenever the mood takes you. Then pass on to the road through crooked and ever-narrowing Barnstable, even to Cape Cod and Race Point. See if you are not inspired by surroundings that whisper of the centuries, that tell of faithful Massasoit, burly Myles Standish, gentle John Alden, and determined Governor Carver, as well as of the dainty Priscilla and a score more of brave women who survived the first deadly winter in the new land.

But if the railroad must be chosen, note should be taken of the fact that there are two routes to Plymouth. It is better to take the longer of the two, for this follows the coast. Yet if it is difficult to decide between them, why not take them both? A down trip to Plymouth by the inland route, and a return trip along the coast is a satisfactory arrangement. Only a few miles separate the roads, but there is a great contrast between them. The shorter road is, much of it, through a country flat and uninteresting in itself, where there is much scrub growth along the way. But the shore line offers views of the bay, and rolling land, and old houses. So what if the trains are slow? Remember that twenty miles an hour would have seemed to the Pilgrims like witchcraft.

The first ten miles of both routes are the same. Naturally the eye turns back across the harbor to South Boston, where, on Dorchester Heights, stands the marble monument that tells of a heroic deed performed when Plymouth was old, yet so long ago that it seems like a legend. Boston was sulking in the hands of the British invaders. Most people thought it was impossible to dislodge them, but the resourceful Washington noted a commanding height that the enemy with all their craft had left unguarded. What could he not do from this, if only he had artillery! A weakling would have balked at that "if only." But Washington was no weakling. By incredible perseverence in the face of obstacles the necessary armament was brought all the way from Ticonderoga, and the first Lord Howe knew of the adventure that meant doom for him was when all was ready for a galling fire that would make his situation untenable. Wisely he did not wait for the event, but decided that discretion was the better part of valor, and withdrew.

The best view of Dorchester Heights is from the Great Blue Hill, back of Milton, the highest point of the range that rears aloft so unexpectedly, within a short distance of the bay, and so close to Boston that it is included in the Metropolitan Park System.

The Great Blue Hill, rising six hundred and thirty-five feet above the tide, is the highest spot on the entire North Atlantic Coast south of Mount Desert. There Harvard has its Meteorological Observatory. And what a chance there is for observations! Forty miles to the north is revealed Cape Ann, the extreme point of Massachusetts Bay. It is sixty miles to Mount Monadnock, but this height may be seen in favorable weather, as well as some of the peaks across the line in New Hampshire. To the south appears Plymouth, nearly forty miles away. It is a prospect that should be seen; it will add to the joy of life.

In 1894 Massachusetts set apart the Blue Hill Reservation of more than four thousand acres, that there might no longer be danger of the destruction of the crowding trees on the slopes and that the people might have freedom to climb above the mists and the dust of the lowlands and breathe the purer air and so gain courage for renewing the contest with the world down among men.

Milton itself is a good foil to the Reservation, with its old houses and streets where the trees, set at a dignified distance apart by the hands of the men of

62

THE ADAMS HOUSES, QUINCY, MASSACHUSETTS

THE QUINCY HOUSE, QUINCY, MASSACHUSETTS
Erected 1706

long ago, seem determined to approach one another aloft in most lover-like fashion.

Quincy, just beyond Milton, at the eastern edge of the seven-mile stretch of the Blue Hills, was one of the landing-places of Captain John Smith in 1614. On his map he called the place London, for, though there was no town there, he felt sure it would one day be the scene of a great settlement. His map was, in a sense, prophetic, for, while a metropolis did not spring up there, great men throve in the locality. John Hancock was born in the neighborhood, and so were two presidents of the United States, John Adams and John Quincy Adams.

The houses in which the two presidents lived are still standing, close together, and at an angle that will not be forgotten by those who have seen them. One seems a very ordinary affair; the other has a roof sloping abruptly from the peak to the rear. The house is two stories and a half high at the summit, but the roof drops so that from the eaves a man could almost reach the ground by hanging at arm's length.

The staid history of communities along this stretch of New England coast is varied by Weymouth, the township with its many villages where Thomas Weston first settled in 1622. His followers were such roystering, irreligious troublemakers that their more serious neighbors to the south breathed a sigh of relief when they proposed to seek again the darker haunts of London from which they had come. The Pilgrims were so eager for this ebb in the immigration movement that they found means to assist it, though their own pockets were all but empty.

Their joy over the departure of the trouble-makers

with the Indians of Wessagusset did not last long; the coming of later colonists showed them that they had made progress from the frying pan into the fire. Captain Wollaston, who, in 1625, brought a company of irresponsible traders to Wollaston Hill, was bad enough. Fortunately these soon sought the more genial climate of the south. After them there descended upon the unsuspecting shore of Massachusetts Bay Thomas Morton and his satellites, who grievously offended the serious-minded Pilgrims by their wordly conduct on the height, whose name they changed from Wollaston to Merry Mount. Bradford charged them with conducting "a schoole of atheism." He added: "His men did quaff strong waters and comfort themselves as if they had anew revived and celebrated the feasts of ye Roman Goddess Flora, or the beastly practices of ye mad Bacchanaliaus." To crown their infamy, they set up a maypole, to celebrate the May Day of 1627, and invited the Indians to join them in carousing and dancing about the lofty pine stem, decked in fantastic fashion that appealed to the savages.

The maypole and even the drinking were of minor importance in comparison with the fact that friendship with the Indians was cultivated by improper means. Not only did the leader at Merry Mount give them drink, but he supplied them with arms and ammunition. The Pilgrim band remonstrated with Morton, reminding him that the proclamation of the king made in 1622 forbade such practices.

Finally the patience of those who saw their safety endangered was exhausted. In 1628 Myles Standish was sent to Merry Mount to arrest the trouble-maker. The doughty captain was not dismayed when Morton

DEERFIELD VALLEY, WEST DEERFIELD, MASSACHUSETTS

offered to shoot him, but "stept to him, and put up his peece, and took him."

Then followed the first forcible deportation from New England. Morton was taken on board the ship *Whale,* which he later described as "a pitiful, weather-beaten craft," adding that in it he was "in more danger than Jonah in the whales belly." But he survived the voyage and did his best to make trouble in England for those responsible for his deportation.

This ended a series of conflicts with Indians and white men at Weymouth that began in April, 1623, when Standish took with him four men to consult in a small room with as many Indians. The Indians were treacherous, and the white men killed them all. Thus they inspired with a brief respect the followers of the dead men who had made a conspiracy against the whites. The incident is noteworthy, not only because of the temporary suppression of the Indians, but because of the unconscious humor of Pastor Robinson of Plymouth, who thought that it would have been sufficient to kill two of the four Indians.

On the road to Weymouth Standish sometimes paused at Hingham, one of the oldest settlements in Plymouth Colony, where today the drives are memorable because of a wealth of shade and many old houses. But the central feature of the community is the Old Ship Church, not far from the railroad station. The organization dates from 1635, and the present building was raised on three July days in 1681. Numerous attempts have been made to change the old structure, whose quaintly pitched roof is responsible for its name, but always the decision has been reached to retain the old distinctive lines.

Not so far from the historic Hingham rises Captain's
Hill in Duxbury where, in 1631, Captain Myles Standish
settled on the one-hundred-and-fifty-acre farm where
he spent the remainder of his days, except when he was
called away by the needs of the colonists. They had
learned to depend on him during the sorrows of the
first winter, when he was one of the seven men who
cared for the sick and dying and helped to guard the
little company at Plymouth. When he went to Duxbury
the women breathed more freely because he promised
to respond to any call for aid.

John Alden lived close by with the Priscilla whom
he courted in vain for his friend. Husband and wife
are buried near the scenes they loved. The grave of
Standish is marked by a stone parapet on which four
guns are mounted. Rising high above Captain's Hill
is the granite monument, surmounted by a twelve-foot
bronze statue of Standish in full uniform. The corner-stone was laid in 1872. It rises one hundred and
ten feet above the two-hundred-foot hill, and so is
the most prominent landmark in all the historic
neighborhood. Within easy reach of the monument
is the house built by Standish's son in 1666, ten years
after the captain's death.

From the top of the monument there is a breath-
taking view. Eighteen miles away, across the bay, is
the tip of Cape Cod. To the right lies Plymouth, with
its green hills, on one of which stands the Pilgrim
Monument, the largest granite monument in the world,
crowned by the representation of Faith, thirty-six feet
high, above four seated figures that represent Morality,
Education, Law and Freedom—the principles upon
which the Pilgrims founded the commonwealth. Near

THE ALDEN HOUSE, DUXBURY, MASSACHUSETTS

THE STANDISH HOUSE, DUXBURY, MASSACHUSETTS
Erected 1666

SAND DUNES, PROVINCETOWN, MASSACHUSETTS

the foot of the hill, in Kingston, is the house built by members of the Bradford family in 1675. Across the nearest reach of water is the long spit of Duxbury Beach, with Saquish Head at the point and the twin lighthouses of the Gurnet just beyond.

From Duxbury a bridge spans the marshes to the strange projecting beach which encloses Clark's Island between itself and the mainland. The trip to the island should be made, if possible, for this is the memorable spot where the eighteen men in the shallop of the *Mayflower* landed on the night of Saturday, December 20, 1620. They had left the ship at Provincetown in search of a suitable place for the settlement of the waiting Pilgrims.

From a large rock on the island, which now bears the inscription 'On the Sabbath Day we rested,' the first prayer was offered, it is said, on New England shores. The next day the Pilgrims of the shallop sailed over to the mainland, and decided that there the *Mayflower* should come and the first settlement should be made.

At last the visitor is ready for Plymouth itself. Whether his entry is by rail or by highway he will come to the prosperous town by Court Street, passing Memorial Hall with its priceless relics of the brave men and women of long ago, and looking up to the hills which first attracted the ship-weary seekers for religious liberty. The last of these hills is Burial Hill —one hundred and sixty-five feet high. The usual approach to this historic cemetery is by the steps at the head of Leyden Street, between the churches. But some think it is better to enter from the rear, making of the impressive entrance an exit on the way to the memorable Rock.

While there are on Burial Hill no stones that date from the earlier years of the settlement of the colony, there is abundant interest for the reverent stroller. Many of the oldest stones are framed in protecting galvanized iron, while one—the oldest original stone— is set in the heart of a modern granite slab.

Burial Hill offers one of the finest views of the Bay, bounded on the left by the height where looms the Standish monument. In front is the long sand spit that reaches back to the uplands. To one side is Manomet, the famous height where Massasoit sometimes conferred with his friends the colonists.

The steps from Burial Hill lead to "the oldest street in New England," Leyden Street, where grow the famous lindens. The Pilgrims came by way of Holland, where the linden is a favorite tree.

Not far away is Coles Hill, the original burial ground where, during the first winter, the graves were dug for half the colony. No stones marked their resting place, for the survivors, facing the attacks of Indians who might learn of their weakness, planted the ground with corn.

The way to the Rock is down the street that leads to the water front, past dismal stores of foreigners who have followed in the steps of the fathers. For a time the stone rested, after many adventures, above the tide, under a canopy that inspired as much ridicule as the relic inspired reverence. But a part of the plan for the Tercentenary Celebration of 1920 was the removal of the relic to tide level, and the erection above it of a simple marble portico.

FROM BOSTON TO CAPE COD

Now for Cape Cod and Provincetown, where the Pilgrims first landed. Here is the eighteen-mile section where a good highway urges the traveler to forsake the roundabout railroad. Those who do not do so will miss an easy chance to go to Billington Sea and the Great South Pond, to the right of Manomet, one of which was probably the "Great Pond" to which Carver and his companions went on that day in early March, when they were in search of evidence of the spring that was to end the cruel winter of 1620.

Near the close of the eighteen-mile gap between Plymouth and the Cape Cod Canal—a canal cut to fulfill the long-standing dream of an easy passage from Boston to the waters of Long Island Sound—is Sagamore Beach, with its wonderful spring of fresh water. A little farther on is Sandwich, where Standish once came near losing his life. With some companions, he had gone south of Plymouth in search of corn. An Indian who wished to murder him, urged him to lie down and sleep. But the wise captain insisted that he "had no desire to rest," and the Indian was fooled.

The southern shore of Cape Cod is an interesting place. The scenery may not amount to much, but think of the associations! It is said that Squanto, the friend of the Pilgrims, is buried on Pleasant Bay in Harwich, for there he died after asking Governor Bradford to pray that his spirit might go to the "white man's God."

And southeast of Harwich is a dread region which has seen disaster for hundreds of years. There, it is held by many, were the " wonderstrands " on which Eric the Norseman more than nine hundred years ago broke the keel of his ship. A modern visitor to the spot declares that these "wonderstrands" were the "dan-

gerous shoals'' of Bradford's history, which alone
prevented the settlement of the Pilgrims south of New
England. "Today they would not divert the voyage
of the *Mayflower,* for Monomoy Point, which now runs
as a long sand spit due south for seven miles, is
composed of the same material that in 1620 made
out in a long point running due east. The Pilgrims
returned to Provincetown simply because Monomoy
then pointed east."

From Monomoy and Chatham and Orleans the
curving peninsula pursues its sandy way a little north
of west to Princetown and Cape Cod. Thoreau
called this last section of the peninsula "the bared
and bended arm of Massachusetts."

And it is bare. There is sand in hills, sand in
windrows, sand everywhere. Rock is all but unknown,
so that brick must be used for foundations. Thoreau,
in his famous study of Cape Cod, noticed the fact that
vessels are forbidden to take stone from the beach for
ballast, and that the crews will sometimes land at night
to steal them.

Captain John Smith preceded the Pilgrims to the
peninsula. In his "New England" he spoke of it as
"only a headland of high hills of sand, overgrowne
with shrubbie pines, brush and such trash, but an
excellent harbour for all weathers. The Cape is made
by the Maine sea on the one side and a great Bay on
the other, in the form of a sickle."

When the weary visitors from Holland came to
Provincetown they saw "a goodly land" which was
"wooded to the brinke of the sea."

Four days later a party went ashore, guided by
Myles Standish, and explored the country. They had

70

gone but a mile when they met a number of Indians and a "dogg." The explorers kept on their way until they came to the place where the town of Truro now is. Here they saw "new stubble where corne had been set ye same year; also they found where lately a house had been where some planks and a great kettle were remaining and heaps of sand newly paddled with their hands, which they, digging up, found in them diverse fine Indian basket filled with corne."

On November 17 when they returned to the *Mayflower*, it was necessary to "wade above the knees." The exposure had fatal effects. "Some of our people that are dead took the original of their deaths here," wrote Governor Bradford later.

Provincetown was not settled until 1680, and the name it now bears was not given to it until 1727. Nearly two centuries later the monument commemorating the first landing of the Pilgrims on the site of the town was built on a sandy hillock, the only eminence near. Two hundred and fifty feet high it stands, proclaiming to all who approach the shore that here was the real beginning of American liberty.

CHAPTER X

THROUGH THE HEART OF THE BERKSHIRES

THE traveler who has chosen any one of the many routes through the famous Berkshire Hills is apt to declare that his is the best way of approach. And it is difficult to disprove his statement, since, however approached, the Berkshire country is surpassingly beautiful. The chosen route may be from Springfield, by railroad along the narrow Westfield River, directly to Pittsfield, and then north. It may be by the turnpike which leaves the route of the railroad, ambles over to Lenox, and then approaches Pittsfield.

Another favorite route is by the automobile road from Canaan over the state line in Connecticut, or by the parallel Berkshire Street Railway. This follows the valley of the Housatonic to Pittsfield, with points of great interest everywhere, passing a dozen summits approaching two thousand feet high. Historic Great Barrington looks off to the east to two of these summits, and to the west to the Dome of the Taconics. This town was once the home of William Cullen Bryant, who was town clerk there.

Two miles to the right of the road, and across the river, rises October Mountain, one of the highest summits south of Pittsfield, where William C. Whitney had his estate, there he had fourteen thousand acres of primeval forest, and there kept numbers of buffalo, elk, deer, moose and antelope.

To the east of October Mountain is Lenox, noted for the magnificent estates of famous Americans, and for the fact that there Nathaniel Hawthorne wrote "The House of Seven Gables," in a house still standing, while Henry Ward Beecher and James Russell Lowell liked to go there when vacation-time called them.

Two more literary sites help to make the region noteworthy. Near the junction of Sackett Brook with the Housatonic, Oliver Wendell Holmes used to spend his summers on the Wendell estate. The lone pine tree celebrated in one of his poems stands near the road. Not two miles away, within the limits of Pittsfield, is the house once owned by the father-in-law of Longfellow, where stood "The Old Clock on the Stairs."

Pittsfield may be entered from the west also by a route directly from the Catskills, through Hudson, on the river of the same name. Between Hudson and Chatham is some of the best of New York's rural scenery. The hills and valleys of this section are not well known, because no through route goes that way. But why think of through routes when, by taking a few hours extra, it is possible to go through country of ever-varying charm? Who could ask for anything better than a summer day of leisurely passing from Hudson to Chatham, from Chatham to Pittsfield, and from Pittsfield to North Adams?

How pleasant it is to watch the hills grow larger, and more commanding! How like a discoverer the traveler feels as one by one Nature lays fresh treasures before him! What if others have preceded him over the road? What if he has been told what he will see? No telling is like the reality; no description can be as good as looking on the masterpieces where forest and meadow vie with tinkling brook and verdant mountain-side to make necessary independent investigation.

Canaan, the New York town close to the border, has an appetizing name. In a valley, girded about by long slopes, it looks like a land flowing with milk and honey. Now and then the railroad cuts through one of the rock-ribbed hills. Did you ever stand on the rear platform on entering such a tunnel, and watch the receding landscape through the portal? Perhaps you think that there cannot be another scene as pleasing as that you are leaving behind. But when you are well on the other side of the tunnel, there is a valley that is even easier to look at; a fresh circle of hills bounds you as in an amphitheatre which opens only to disclose another series of bounding ridges beyond.

In Pittsfield the view is from a height instead of from the valley. The Park, the center of city life, is on an eminence, from which the tree-embowered streets slope away to the valley. Each one of these streets looks so inviting that it is not easy to choose which to follow first. But before leaving the Park it is best to pause at the First Congregational Church, which stands on the site of the church from which "Fighting Parson Allen" led the men of Berkshire to the battle of Bennington.

It is difficult to realize that the neighborhood of Berkshire is not a well-kept park. But it is open country where trees and meadows and lakes are framed in mountains that become always more insistent in their claims to attention.

At length the crowning glory of the Massachusetts mountains is in sight. Old Greylock, 3505 feet high, looms huge behind the town of Adams. The vivid green of its eastern slope is broken by a bare strip which marks the course of a great landslide. To the east rise the lower slopes of the Hoosac Mountains, but the eye turns from them and lingers on the giant to the west, which—so geologists say—is one of the oldest mountains in the world. Once, they claim, the summit was nearly twice as high as it is today; it has been lowered by the sweeping down of great masses of rock to the Green River and so to the sea.

The prospect from this roof of Massachusetts is impressive. On a clear day the eye takes in the country for one hundred to two hundred miles in all directions. To the west, across Green River valley, is the main range of the Taconics. To the northeast is Raven Rock Peak, which is joined to Greylock by Bellows' Pipe Park, a belt of pasture land at an elevation of more than two thousand feet.

Greylock is the monument of Grey Lock, the Woronoak chieftian who died in 1724. On the summit, where he delighted to climb, there has been set apart the Greylock Park Reservation. The beginning of this Reservation was made in 1885, when an association of public-spirited men and women subscribed twenty thousand dollars for the purchase of four hundred acres of land. After building a road from North Adams to the summit, the association agreed with the state to make its holdings a part of the ten thousand acre reservation made by Massachusetts for the lasting pleasure of mountain lovers.

Both North Adams and Williamstown have a claim to Greylock. For generations the climb to the summit has been a privilege held out to visitors. The students and professors of Williams College have made it a place of pilgrimage. The first observatory tower was built by a company of men from college about 1830. William Cullen Bryant was among the students who haunted its forest-clad slopes; inspiration for many of his poems came to him while in these lofty surroundings. It is a tradition in the college town that he composed "Thanatopsis" while walking along Flora's Glen, now known as Thanatopsis Glen. Nathaniel Hawthorne spoke of the visits toward Greylock as a day-dream, while Thoreau wrote, " It would be no small advantage if every college were thus located at the base of a mountain, as good at least as one well-endowed professorship." Perhaps the proximity of the mountain had an influence on the students whose enthusiasm for the world led to the birth of American Missions, as commemorated by the Haystack Monument in the old college town.

The railroad station at North Adams, just below an overhanging bare granite slope, is the point of departure for the next wonder of the neighborhood, the Hoosac Tunnel, whose four and three-quarter miles make it the longest tunnel in America. When it was completed, it was the longest in the world, with the exception of the Mount Cenis tunnel.

Two summits of the Hoosacs long stood in the way of transportation from the valley of the Connecticut to the valley of the Hudson; to the east was a barrier fourteen hundred and fifty feet high, while to the west was another three hundred feet higher. Between the mountains was a valley nearly one thousand feet high.

In 1825 daring men first proposed the cutting of a tunnel for a canal from Boston to the Hudson, but the beginning was not made until 1856. Progress was slow, for at first all work was done by hand drills. Oliver Wendell Holmes once said that the millennium would arrive before its completion. But all difficulties were overcome, and the great work was finally completed by the state in 1874, after the expenditure of fourteen million dollars, and the loss of nearly two hundred lives. The invention of nitro-glycerine, the power drill, and the compressed air drill made possible what long seemed impossible. To the amazement even of the engineers there was a variation of but five-sixteenths of an inch between the heading driven from the east and that which approached it from the west.

Where the railroad emerges from the tunnel it follows a winding, funnel-like passage for miles by the side of the Deerfield River as it dashes enticingly over the stones and among fantastic bowlders. Soon the country opens out and the valley broadens. As the miles pass the stream flows more sedately, yet it is still amid the rocks, and there is such variety that no one dares to say that the end of the turbid part of the river has been reached. All the way to the junction with the Connecticut it has surprises for the saunterer on its banks—here a cool aisle among the arching trees, there a long sweep across the meadows, again a game of hide and seek with the playful rocks, or, in more serious mood, it lingers in the deep pools above a power dam that turns the busy spindles. Thus it makes ready for the strenuous company it will keep on the way from Greenfield to Long Island Sound.

CHAPTER XI

FROM LONG ISLAND TO NANTUCKET

A PASSENGER who hailed from New Haven was leaning on the rail of a Long Island Sound steamer. Silently he looked toward the winding shore of Long Island, and the green fields beyond. Then came a sigh and a shaking of the head.

"New York should never have claimed Long Island," he explained. "By every right it belongs to Connecticut. It was a part of Connecticut, until an arm of the sea rushed in and separated them. And still it is closer to Connecticut than it is to New York—all except the western end where the city has reached out its greedy tentacles to take in Brooklyn. Then Connecticut colonized much of it. You know that in 1643 settlers went over from Stamford to the north shore, settling on land bought from the Indians, and that in 1640 men from Lynn, Massachusetts, made homes on Peconic Bay. In 1662 the new Colony of Connecticut claimed authority over eastern Long Island. And then we lost it!"

Again he shook his head sadly. Evidently he was thinking of Far Rockaway and Great South Bay, of Montauk and Shelter Island, of the Peconic Bay that pierces from the east into the interior of the island, of Long Beach and Oyster Bay, of Cold Spring Harbor and its interesting Biological Laboratory, of the rolling meadows and the inlets from the sea that give access for sailboats into the heart of the land. What a wonderful possession for New York, and how delighted Connecticut would be to have it!

Then his eye shifted to the Connecticut shore, and his talk shifted as well. "But we ought not to grudge it to New York, I suppose," he concluded. "We have a wonderful stretch of coast, and, without Long Island, the Empire State would have only the few miles of East River and the bit at the beginning of the Sound."

In 1731 Connecticut did manage to extend her coast line at the expense of her neighbor to the west. That was the year of the final settlement of a long-standing dispute as to the western line of Connecticut. A tract of sixty thousand acres was ceded to New York in exchange for an equivalent on the southwest. Thus history accounts for the awkward lines that make possible the catch question of the schoolmaster who expects people to know that Connecticut is bounded on the south by New York, while New York, in turn is bounded on the south by Connecticut.

Less than twenty miles of Long Island Sound's northern shore was added to the indented coast line of the Nutmeg State. But these twenty miles include picturesque crooks and bends, as well as inlets and islands. There is also included the site of Stamford. So that picturesque city, founded in 1641 by twenty-nine settlers from Wethersfield, and called Rippowam for a few months, would have been—but for the fortunate settlement—within the bounds of New York.

Reluctantly the Indians yielded ground to these early settlers; they were beginning to realize that the white man was destined to rule where for centuries they had hunted and fished.

Only four years before the sale of Rippowam the

dusky owners had an object lesson in the battle which ended the Pequot War; this was fought close to Westport, less than fifteen miles from Stamford. Those who seek the site of the conflict have only to ascend the Westport River a few miles to the region where, instead of a sprawling inlet, it becomes a sedate stream confined closely to regulation banks. Close to the town is a granite block that tells of The Great Swamp Fight July 13, 1637.

Just a little beyond Westport, and close to the sea, is Fairfield, the center of Connecticut's witchcraft delusion. Here four women were indicted. One of these was sentenced to death, but fortunately she escaped one night in 1692.

Much of the shore between Fairfield and Bridgeport Harbor is laid out as Seaside Park, which, Bridgeport boasts, is one of the finest parks in New England. It is a monument to men like P. T. Barnum, the showman, and Nathaniel Wheeler, of sewing machine fame.

Bridgeport rejoices in the fact that the city dates back to 1691, as well as in the marvelous industrial prosperity that began when the first railroad reached the shore of Pequannock in 1840.

The stranger would expect to find another great industrial city at the mouth of the Housatonic River, which brings down to the Sound the flavor of the Berkshires. But Connecticut has so many streams entering the Sound that it could hardly be expected that a town of note would mark the mouth of each of them. In fact, there are so many of these streams that there is a singular paucity of names. For instance, in the forty-mile stretch from Stamford to New Haven there are three Mill Rivers!

New Haven has a majestic approach from the Sound. The wide sweep of New Haven Bay leads to the sentinel East Rock and its companion West Rock, each close to four hundred feet high, which guard the city on either side. Far beyond the city there is another landmark for which the navigator learns to look—the West Peak of the Hanging Hills, near Southington, twenty-five miles away, the southern terminus of the range of volcanic hills which come down from the north.

Once the Sound reached far up toward the hills; both Mill River and Quinnipiac River flow between banks that have risen above the surface of the waters, then branches of the sea.

These natural waterways did not satisfy aspiring New Haven. In the early years of the nineteenth century, longing for some of the trade from the north that was coming to the Sound by way of navigable streams, the town joined hands with Farmington and other communities up the state in constructing the Farmington Canal, which eventually led to Northampton in Massachusetts. There was great excitement when, in 1835, the twenty-eight locks in Connecticut and the thirty-two locks in Massachusetts were thrown open, and boats like the *Wild-fire* moved serenely along the "Raging Canawl," at the speed of from two-and-a-half to even five miles an hour. But the locks were the death of the improvement—there were so many of them and the expense of building and maintaining them was so great, that the artificial waterway could not pay expenses, and it gave way to the railroad.

So New Haven lost her canal. But she still has her famous Green, a social center that is to New Haven what the Common is to Boston. In 1638, when the town was founded, the Green was set apart, and for nearly three hundred years it has witnessed the joys and the sorrows of passing generations. There the first elm trees were planted in 1686. There Whitefield preached in the brooding shade of the trees. There indignant citizens gathered to hurl anathemas at the authors of the iniquitous Stamp Act. There citizens strolled along the criss-cross paths on the way to the churches whose steeples rose among the bordering trees, and since then visitors have loitered in reluctance to leave the charmed spot. For more than two hundred years Yale students have made pilgrimage from the old Quadrangle to the open space that has meant as much to the city on the Sound as the Old Fence has meant to the seniors who were privileged to sit on its top rail.

Yearly the center of Yale interest is transferred from New Haven along the Sound, past the mouth of the Connecticut at Saybrook, first seat of the College, past Hatchett's Point and Niantic Bay, to New London and the Thames River. For there the stage is set for the annual contest with Harvard for the mastery of the racing shells. Gales Ferry, eight miles from New London, the chosen headquarters for the Yale crews, is a lively place for a few weeks before the racing season.

Within easy distance of the mouth of the Thames is Block Island, whose story dates at least as far back as 1636, when vengeance came down from the Connecticut River on Indian murderers of John Oldham, trader to the bleak and barren Block Island, that looks like an outcast from its neighbor, Long

82

MEANDERS OF MILL RIVER IN FOREGROUND; NEW HAVEN,
CONNECTICUT, IN BACKGROUND

ROCKY SHORE ON THE SOUTH SIDE OF BLOCK ISLAND

Island. Connecticut was not able to lay hands even on this rugged outpost of a stormswept coast, though Massachusetts, the parent of Connecticut, asserted authority over the murderous Indians by demanding a penalty of four fathoms of wampum. Rhode Island, heir to the interests of Massachusetts, rules over Block Island and the small company of those who find a living among the salt ponds, the rocks, and the marshes which yearly attract so many summer pilgrims.

Block Island bears the name of the Dutch explorer, Adrian Block, who visited these waters in 1614, though the Dutch map of the next few years called it Adrian's Eyland. Verazzano, who explored the island in 1624, attempted to call it Claudia, but he was unsuccessful in making the name of his choice persist. In the account of his visit he called attention to the hills in terms a little more complimentary than the modern writer who says: "It is doubtful whether a more uneven surface on the earth can be pointed out. No person ever saw the surface of the ocean more uneven than is Block Island, excepting those who survived the flood in the days of Noah."

The description may be more or less true of parts of the island, but there are other portions where easy roads wind attractively among the fertile green fields.

In 1660 sixteen men became purchasers of these uneven acres by payment of £400. Later the island became the refuge of deserters in time of war who found among the bogs and marshes a secure hiding place. And it was long the haunt of wreckers who lured ships on the rocks for the sake of pillage. In "The Palatine" Whittier has related the legend of

one famous wreck on what he called Manisees, the
Indian name for the island:

> "Leagues north, as fly the gull and auk,
> Point Judith watches with eye of hawk;
> Leagues south, thy beacon flame, Montauk!

> "Circled by waters that never freeze,
> Beaten by billow and swept by breeze,
> Lieth the island of Manisees.

> "Set at the mouth of the Sound to hold
> The coast lights up on its turret old,
> Yellow with moss and sea fog mould."

"Leagues north of Block Island," Point Judith
reaches out toward the Atlantic, one of the most
prominent headlands on Rhode Island's four hundred
miles of seacoast. It is difficult to believe that there
is so much of the coast, for the state is only fifty per
cent larger than the Okefinokee Swamp in Georgia.
But the various passages of Narragansett Bay, studded
by islands that are simply beautiful and others that
are wonderfully beautiful, afford hidden opportunities
of which the searching surf takes full advantage.

Point Judith was a landmark of the Narragansett
Country, which extended to East Greenwich on the
north and to the Pawcatuck River on the west. The
river, by the way, is of more prominence in history than
its size would indicate, for it figured in the boundary
controversy with Connecticut. The Nutmeg State held
that the Narragansett River which formed her eastern
boundary was Narragansett Bay. The counter-claim
was that Pawcatuck River was the real Narragansett
River. Fortunatly for Rhode Island, Connecticut's
claim did not hold. Fortunately also for Rhode Island,

the state has other streams even more picturesquely named. For instance, there is the Pettaquamscutt, the Saugatucket, the Chepuxit, and the Sakonet!

The southern border of the Narragansett Country is bounded on the west by Watch Hill, whose beach at the mouth of the Pawcatuck is sought by eager tourists, while it is bounded on the east by famous Narragansett Pier. Between the two resorts stretches an almost continuous sandy beach bounded on the south by the ocean, on the north by salt water marshes. Once Indians sought the sea on these beaches, and today their white successors come by thousands to swim and fish, or it may be merely to take long, satisfied looks at sky and water, or back to the land where swamps and hills lead up to the highest eminence in the state—Durfee Hill, more than eight hundred feet above the sea.

Back among those hills and ponds, as well as along the shores of Narragansett Bay, were the old plantations of the days of slavery in Rhode Island, where, Thomas Wentworth Higginson declared, are remains of old houses that recall the feudal system better than any other relics in America.

In keeping with the leisurely life of other days is the modern life at Narragansett Pier, with its bright lights and it gay throngs, its spirited assemblages on the beach and in the casino, its shore walk with water on one side and green lawns sloping to houses called cottages, though many of them are more like palaces.

The entrance to Narragansett Bay is north of the Pier—rather, the entrances, for both Conanicut Island and Rhode Island are obstacles in the way of the sea. The intricate shore line made problems for the old slave traders who sought Newport Harbor before the Revolution, as today they increase the pleasure of the yachtsmen who sail the waters of the bay.

Rhode Island is the largest of the many islands in the archipelago of the state to which it gave its name. The Indians called it Aquidneck, "Isle of Peace." Verazzano in 1524 disregarded this title and called it Luisa. At the same time he compared it to the Island of Rhodes in the Mediterranean. That comparison fixed the name of the gem of Narragansett, called by a historian of 1715 "the paradise of New England," which was "a coat warmer" than Boston, though it was but sixty-five miles away. This difference is due to the Gulf Stream, which is closer to Rhode Island than it is to Boston.

When the British left Newport in 1779 the town was in ruins. "But I doubt not the town will be rebuilt and exceed its former splendor," one historian of the day wrote. It has been rebuilt, but with different splendor; in the old days it was a seaport, with docks a mile long, and it even aspired to be the metropolis of America. Today it is a resort pre-eminent in the opinion of many who find there a restful combination of towering cliff and boiling surf, of green hills and shady streets, of blue water dotted with the white sails of speedy yachts, of walks that are quiet and peaceful and other walks that are close to the noise and confusion of the tireless sea, of forts and lighthouse and windmills.

Among the windmills of the island many thoughtful people count the Old Stone Mill in Touro Park which has been the subject of more speculation perhaps than any other relic in America. Longfellow made his guess

THE CLIFF WALK, NEWPORT, RHODE ISLAND

FIRST BAPTIST CHURCH, PROVIDENCE, RHODE ISLAND
Erected 1774

as to this ruin when he wrote "The Skeleton in Armor."
He connected the town with the Northmen, and made
one of them say:

> "There, for my lady's bower,
> Built I the lofty tower,
> Which to this very hour,
> Stands looking seaward."

But romance has been pricked effectively by a study
of the will of Benedict Arnold, the first charter governor of the colony, who referred several times to "My
Stone Built Wind Mill," and in such a manner
that its identity with the Round Tower on the hill
seems certain.

There is an old town in Newport, and there is a new
town. But it is the old town that demands the closest
attention, with its Trinity Church on the hill, its
Washington Square, its State House, dating from 1738,
and its numerous old houses that speak so eloquently
of the days when James Fenimore Cooper wrote "The
Red Rover."

Of all the walks about Newport many find greatest
charm in the Cliff Walk, three and one half miles long,
with the sea far below on the one hand, while on the
other tower the summer cottages and palaces of those
whose love for Newport has led them to the heights.
Others prefer to go toward Sachuest Beach, passing
on the way Purgatory, a yawning chasm in the rocky
promontory where waves tumble and crash and pound,
as if in ceaseless rage for the legendary lover to whom
a heedless girl once said, "Jump the chasm if you
would claim my hand." The sequel says that the lover
jumped successfully across the gap—which is eight

feet wide at its narrowest place—and then walked disdainfully away, determined never again to look on the face of the heartless woman.

These sea-swept islands where the surf beats ceaselessly were so attractive both to Massachusetts and Plymouth Bay Colonies that both laid claim to them, until far into the eighteenth century. Plymouth tried to retain hold of the region east of the Sakonnet, but in 1746 she yielded her claim to Cumberland, Warren, Bristol, Tiverton and Little Compton.

Across from Tiverton is Portsmouth, a town that claims greater age than Newport, for there was the first settlement made in Rhode Island. But Bristol, across the channel on the mainland, claims to be older by hundreds of years. There, her people assert, was the site of the Vinland of the Norsemen, who sailed up the Sakonnet River about the year 1000.

Following the lure of picturesque waters, the modern successor to the visitors from Plymouth goes on past Bristol, where the privateers gathered during the War of 1812, up Providence River to Providence, which became a rival of Newport more than one hundred and fifty years ago. The founding of the institution that became Brown University gave prominence to the act of the famous Providence Athenæum, the library, thrown open in 1753, which ordered that "whenever the General Assembly meets in Providence the Librarian...shall deliver to whomsoever they appoint the Keys of the Library...so that the members may have opportunity to read any of the books if they see Cause, trusting to their Honor to leave them in their Place."

The waters that lead from Providence back to the

open ocean are left behind reluctantly by the traveler who is studying the wonders of the New England coast. "I am coming this way again," he is apt to promise himself, before he faces forward to Buzzard's Bay, with New Bedford, of whale-ship fame, on the left, the Elizabeth Islands on the right, and in between the ships whose navigators rejoice in the Cape Cod Canal that has enabled them to cut off many miles of tempestuous sailing around the long coast line of Barnstable.

South of Barnstable lies a strange but delightful group of islands which look on the map like remnants of the lower jaw of an elephant whose upper jaw and uplifted trunk is formed by Barnstable, whose gaping mouth is Nantucket Sound, guarded by Monomoy Island and Great Point, the teeth; whose throat passage is Vineyard Sound. The Elizabeth Islands form one side of this passage, while the other side is formed by Martha's Vineyard. The latter island stretches away to the east where Muskeget Channel and Muskeget and Tuckermuck Islands show where once must have been solid land that connected the Vineyard and Nantucket. The similarity of vegetation on the two islands that form the southern frontier of Massachusetts helps to confirm the idea that in the days of long ago they were one.

Imaginary? Perhaps. But the indescribable charm of Martha's Vineyard is anything but imaginary. Whether the traveler approaches its shore from Newport or from Wood's Hole, through Vineyard Sound, or comes past No Man's Land and the southern shore where the waves from the broad Atlantic sweep without restraint on a beach twenty miles long, he will

have to own that here, at last, is "something different."
He may be travel-weary, but his weariness will depart
magically. He may have been an unbeliever in the
possibility that there can be anything worth while on
such an outpost, out in the ocean, but he will learn
his error very promptly. He may be one of the
tiresome individuals who insist that it is impossible
to take a vacation; but Martha's Vineyard will make
him regret the years when he was foolishly insistent
on working without a break.

What can a man do in Martha's Vineyard? He
can wander on the beach, or stand on the heights which
are like box seats for the unexampled show of the
shipping that moves swiftly to and fro along the marine
lane connecting Baltimore, Philadelphia, and Boston;
he can trudge back among the smiling farmlands or seek
the ponds, some salt, some fresh; he can go to the
picturesque towns like Vineyard Haven and Edgartown,
whose streets were laid out by the seafaring men who
built them; he can seek the heaths where the dancing
heath hen makes her last stand in America; he can
fish, and he can sail, and he can swim. There is really
no limit to what he can do—his trouble will be that
he has not allowed himself time enough to taste all
the pleasures of the miniature territory perched
superbly across the path of those who skirt the lower
New England Coast.

Nantucket Island may not be so large as Martha's
Vineyard, but it has even more of the atmosphere of
the sea. For one thing, it is farther from the mainland. Then it was settled two hundred and seventy
years ago by Yankee salts whose descendants—some
of them bearing the original names—are anchored for

WHALING VESSEL *CHARLES W. MORGAN*, DOCKED AT NANTUCKET, MASSACHUSETTS
After Twenty-seven Months' Cruise

NORTH BLUFF, MARTHA'S VINEYARD, MASSACHUSETTS

always on the land that owes its being to the Indian giant Mashopen, who formed it by emptying the ashes of his pipe into the sea. At least that is the tale the Indians used to recount. Then, as if in childish pleasure at their story-telling genius, they go on to say that the giant, satisfied with his labors, used to light his pipe on the island so much that the smoke caused the fogs to cling to the shores.

Some of those early settlers called the island Nantukes. Others wrote the name Nantucquet Isle. But usually, whatever they called it, they clung to it when they lived there, and longed for it when they were absent. Those who have never been there may easily wonder why they were so partial to the long strip of sand with its bays and headlands, its ponds and harbors, its beaches and gently curving shore. But let those who are unwilling to become slaves of the island, keep safely away from it. If they climb the streets of Nantucket, the old whaling town; walk out two miles to the tablet that marks the birthplace of Abiah Folger, mother of Benjamin Franklin; stroll on to Siasconset; remain there long enough to call it 'Sconset; then pass on to Sankaty Head, eighty-five feet above the sea, and look toward far-away Europe, it is almost a certainty that they will be Nantucket converts for life.

Visitors remark the absence of deciduous trees in almost all parts of the "mutton chop" island. The winds blow constantly with great velocity, so that such trees have little chance to grow; they need water, and the wind robs the leaves of moisture more rapidly than the roots can supply it, especially when they grow in a porous soil. But there is a wealth of other vegetation. There are evergreen trees, and there are cranberry bogs. There are heathlands among the rolling hills, which one famous botanist has likened to the Roman Campagna. Here and there are clumps of the huckleberry or the bearberry, whose woody stems, covered with small evergreen, leathery leaves, make a springy surface for the pedestrian, like a Turkish rug. Think of walking on such a carpet, acres and acres of it!

CHAPTER XII

THE VALLEY OF THE CONNECTICUT RIVER

THE Connecticut Valley is a dream come true. There romance and reality join hands in glorious partnership, while beauty and utility unite in satisfying measure. For three hundred and sixty miles—from the Canadian border to Long Island Sound—it is generous with gifts of beauty for those who delight in endless variety of valley and mountain, of water and verdure, of cloud and sunshine.

Here was a favorite hunting ground for the Indian, and a passage way for the braves as they went from the waters of the Sound toward the waters of the St. Lawrence. Then came the Dutch, who preferred their own name, De Versche Riviere (Fresh-water River) to the musical Quoneh-to-cut of the savages. Followed then the courageous settlers from Massachusetts, who made their homes on the banks of the lower river, defying death at the hands of the dispossessed Indians, persisting in their occupation of the chosen lands in spite of barbarous massacres, pushing farther and yet farther north until quarrels with other settlers who wanted the same lands threatened to be almost as disastrous as had been the long continued warfare with the Indians.

But even these pioneers took time from their struggles with nature and with man to revel in the beauty about them. They clung to the banks of the stream, and delighted in building homes in advantageous locations. Their thoughts were given expression more than one hundred years ago by Timothy Dwight in his *Travels in New England*. He declared that this stream "may perhaps with more propriety than any other in the world be named the Beautiful River." Then, in stately sentences, he continued: "The purity, salubrity, and sweetness of its waters; the frequency and elegance of its meanders, its absolute freedom from all aquatic vegetables, the uncommon and unusual beauty of its banks,—here a smooth and winding beach, there covered with rich verdure, now fringed with bushes, now covered with lofty trees, and now formed by the intruding hill, the rude bluff, and the shaggy mountain,—are objects which no traveler can thoroughly describe, and no reader can adequately imagine."

The windings of the Beautiful River lead across Connecticut, the Land of Steady Habits, through the heart of Massachusetts, between the Berkshires and the luscious lands toward the east; then on between the Green Mountains and the White Mountains, where neither New Hampshire nor Vermont has been willing to yield all claim to its bordering banks.

Those who would learn for themselves have ample choice of modes of travel. They can go on the New York boat from the Sound up to Hartford. They may prefer the good road that keeps rather close to the bank most of the way from the mouth far into Vermont. Or they may choose the railroad, breaking the journey at the end of the first day at Springfield and taking passage in the morning for Barnet, Vermont, where the railroad must be abandoned for the road that follows the northeasterly course of the rapidly narrow-

THE VALLEY OF THE CONNECTICUT RIVER

ing stream to the lakes where it has its source, halfway between the borders of Quebec and northern Maine.

Difficult railroad connections along the lower river should not hinder the beginning of the journey at Saybrook where the stream gives "cool hand to the waiting sea." This town preserves the names of Lord Say and Seal and Lord Brook, two of the English company of "Lords and Gentlemen" who came to the mouth of the Connecticut in 1635, having received from the Plymouth Colony in England a charter to territory extending from Narragansett Bay to the Pacific Ocean. Later their generously indefinite rights were transferred to George Fenwick, colonist of 1639, who bravely founded Saybrook above the fort at the mouth of the river, built by the English in 1635 in spite of the fact that two years earlier the Dutch had taken possession of this spot in token of their purpose to control the Connecticut. For some years there was a pretty struggle between the rival claimants to the Connecticut, but eventually the Dutch withdrew.

For five years Fenwick held on grimly. Then he transferred his troublesome claim to the English colonists farther up the river. In the meantime Lady Fenwick died and was buried at Saybrook, where her grave is still pointed out.

Old Saybrook rejoices in the fact that here was the first seat of Yale College, whose removal to New Haven gave the romancing Samuel Peters, in his undependable History of Connecticut, an opportunity to embellish a tale that would have been interesting without trimmings. He declares that "because the people of New Haven and Hartford suspected that Saybrook was not truly Protestant," because it had

95

a passion for the "leeks and onions of Egypt, and because youth belonging to them in the *Schola Illustris* were in great danger of imbibing its lukewarmness," Hartford voted to remove the college to Wethersfield, while New Haven determined to lay hold of the institution for herself. Hartford acted first; a mob went down the river with teams and boats, seized "the college apparatus, library and students, and carried all to Wethersfield."

Not to be outdone, a New Haven mob went to Wethersfield and laid violent hands upon the institution. But they were not so successful, for on the road to the coast they were overtaken by the mob from Hartford, which succeeded in taking back part of the library and students.

Thus it happened that for a time students gathered at Saybrook, Wethersfield, and New Haven. Peace was finally signed, and New Haven won the college, to the joy of Boston, so Peters says, because the decision removed the rival of Harvard College forty miles farther away!

In passing up the river the traveler soon comes to Selden Neck, a beautiful island in part controlled for the people by the Connecticut State Park Commission. The Neck is also a reminder of Saybrook; it was granted in 1650 to John Cullick by the General Court of Hartford, for his services in connection with the union of the town of Saybrook with the Connecticut Colony, farther up the river.

The winding river soon leads to Essex, noted in the Revolution for the building of a ship of war, and in the war of 1812 for the destruction there of American vessels by the British. East Haddam, too,—where the

96

UP SELDEN CREEK, CONNECTICUT RIVER

ON THE CONNECTICUT RIVER

Salmon River enters the Connecticut, flowing between leafy banks,—was once a shipbuilding point. But perhaps a greater claim to fame is the fact that there Nathan Hale taught school before the Revolution.

Haddam, on the west bank of the river, and a little farther up stream, rejoices that it was the birthplace of such famous men as Stephen Johnson Field, Justice of the United States Supreme Court, and of David Brainerd, Apostle to the Indians. Justice Field's father was once pastor in the delightful old town, and his memory is kept green by the park dedicated to him.

Above Haddam the river narrows rapidly, winding amid green forests to Middle Haddam, where it makes the last great bend before reaching away to the north by a course that is remarkably direct, sweeping by little, wooded Dart Island, a microscopic State Park area that has been preserved very nearly as it was when Dutch and English rivals ruled the river.

The residents of Middle Haddam have the privilege of resorting to a much larger area administered by the State Park Commission, Hurd Park, with a river frontage of more than a mile, where Hurd Brook cuts a deep gorge on its way to the river; where forests crown the heights above the water or lead up to eminences still greater which afford unusual views of the fertile lands on both sides; where a dock reaches into the river, the relic of the Hurds who came to the spot about 1710.

After eight miles of varied beauty comes Middletown. Then the river leaves the path of the glacier that ground down through the heart of the Connecticut. The glacier's track, which led on to the site of New Haven, has been marked by Wharton Brook Reservation, a Traveler's Wayside Park close to Wallingford, within easy reach of the great highway from New Haven to Hartford, where arching elms and beeches screen the inviting waters of a stream that looks as if it were miles within a forest.

Middletown on the river has its own near-by height, Great Hill, on whose western slope the state has another of its well-chosen reservations. Within a mile is the highway, and not far distant, is Meshomasick Mountain and the Portland State Forest, one of Connecticut's brave attempts to save its woodland heritage. Close at hand also is the spot where, it is said, John Winthrop found gold.

Middletown has other rugged surroundings. Below the town the river makes its way through what is almost a gorge between high hills. It is not surprising, then, to come on the slopes where the little city is built, and to see the wonderful old trees and the historic houses of the settlement that dates from 1653. Graduates of Wesleyan University look back with delight on the days they spent amid the pleasing surroundings of the town that once threatened the commercial supremacy of Hartford.

Between Middletown and Hartford Wethersfield looks down from its superb location above the river, claiming the admiration of the visitor by the church among the trees, with its tower after Christopher Wren, the old cemetery with its engrossing stones, and the house where Washington stopped, in 1781, making plans with his helpers that were carried out when Cornwallis surrendered his sword at Yorktown. That was long ago, but the town was by no means an infant then. For Wethersfield (then Watertown) was one of three towns planted between 1635 and 1638 by Puritans from Massachusetts, who had been attracted by the fertility of the Connecticut Valley. Together with Hartford and Windsor the town formed the Connecticut colony, backed by a written constitution that was, according to John Fiske, "the true birth of American democracy."

Those who are privileged to see the graceful sweep of river above Wethersfield, who look on the restful trees on either bank that sheltered many houses occupied by descendants of those who helped to shape the early destinies of Connecticut, can understand why the pioneers selected this region for the scene of their home-building achievements, and why the Indians and the Dutch, whom they sought to displace, were reluctant to yield to them.

The Dutch went to the site of Hartford in 1633, ascending the river from the Sound. There followed, overland, the little congregation from Newtown (Cambridge), Massachusetts, led by their pastor, Thomas Hooker. The settlement made on the west bank of the river was known as Newtown until 1637, when it was called Hertford.

Modern Hartford has not hidden by later improvements all reminders of the past. The steamboats land where the boats of the pioneers touched the shore, and disembarking passengers go along many streets whose courses were fixed nearly three hundred years ago. At almost every turn they are faced by landmarks telling of early valor and industry that paved the way for more modern achievements. Chief among these is the marble shaft built where stood the Charter Oak, blown down in 1856, the hiding-place of the royal charter that granted to the colony the right to choose its own government. Those who stand before this memorial think again of that night in 1687 when Sir Edmund Andross, as the king's agent, demanded the charter, only to be foiled by the resourceful men who blew out the candles and spirited away the precious document.

That deed of manly defiance does not stand alone in Hartford's history. Worthy to be noted with it is the narrative of the coming of Governor Fletcher from New York to demand the control of the militia in the king's name. When he insisted on reading the proclamation, he was drummed into silence by command of Wadsworth, the chief officer. The drummer desisted, but the word to him was "Drum, I say," and to the governor, "Stop, sir, or I will make the sun shine through you in an instant."

That narrative is given in the words of Horace Bushnell, whose name is kept alive in Hartford by Bushnell Park, most frequented of the many beautiful recreation areas in the capitol because it is closest to the heart of the city. As thousands enter it daily, they pass through the Memorial Arch erected to the Connecticut soldiers and sailors who served in the Civil War. In the park, on a height, is the Capitol building which has the distinction of being unlike the shrines other states have made for their law-makers; it has a beauty all its own.

Windsor, famous as the third of the original towns of the Connecticut Valley, and the home of one of the early Chief Justices, Oliver Ellsworth, looks over the river to East Windsor Hill, birthplace of Jonathan Edwards. There John Oldham came in 1633, during his exploration of the valley for the Plymouth Colony. His favorable report led to the migration that began the transformation of the region. To him one of the chief attractions of the river, from the point where Windsor is located up to the present northern boundary of Connecticut, was the five-mile section of the Enfield Rapids, where the stream tumbles along a rocky bed. Locks at Windsor and a dam at Enfield bound the rapids and make possible navigation by the Enfield Canal around a difficult bit of stream.

Above the dam the river runs for a time between straitened banks, but just beyond the line, in Massachusetts, it spreads out until it is more than two thousand feet wide. The descent is so gradual that this broad reach looks more like a lake than a river.

Springfield, not far from this notable section of river, has the distinction of having one of the oldest bridges along the Connecticut—a covered bridge, built in 1816, whose massive timbers promise to last much longer than the spirit of progress will permit the structure to remain. Already a projected modern bridge threatens the destruction of the relic, which is still known as the Old Toll Bridge, though it has been free for more than half a century.

Another landmark that may have to yield the proud position it has long occupied in the center of the city is the old First Church, with its distinctive New England tower. "But the loss will not be so great," a resident said to the author. "It was not built until 1817, for it followed three other structures that housed the congregation after its organization in 1637.'' This was the year after the settlement of the town.

Yet it is difficult to think of condemning Springfield for the possible removal of the landmark, since this seems an essential part of the plan for beautifying and enlarging historic Court Square, from early years the center of Springfield life, noted, among other reasons, because some thrilling chapters of Shays' Rebellion were staged beneath its elms.

The fatality that has pursued many of the lordly elms of Connecticut has not passed by the trees of Court Square. Yet a number of the largest still survive. One of these is more than nineteen feet in circumference.

Overlooking the elms from the west side of the square are the twin city buildings, two Corinthian-columned marble structures, one for the business offices, the other an auditorium seating four thousand people. Between these structures rises the lofty, graceful Campanile. Visitors are invited to use the elevator in ascending for the view of river and valley for many miles. What an end such a vision is to a tour of some of the beauty spots of Springfield, especially glorious Forest Park, on the rolling ground above the Connecticut!

''Just think what this country must have been when the Indians were here!'' were the words of the author's companion on the tour of the park. ''They knew how to keep the country looking its best. We have been spoiling it ever since we got it. The fish and game are all but gone, and most of the trees, the wonderful trees that were a benediction to the whole countryside, have been destroyed. We are trying to

MUNICIPAL BUILDINGS AND CAMPANILE, SPRINGFIELD, MASSACHUSETTS

MILLER'S RIVER AT ROYALSTON, MASSACHUSETTS

repair damages here in the park. See what a bird sanctuary this is coming to be!"

King Philip and his men had a vision of the destruction of their hunting grounds when, in 1675, they went on the war path and ravaged the valley from Springfield to Northfield. October 5 was the fatal day for Springfield, when fire destroyed the town, and the inhabitants fled in terror. At the time it looked as if the settlement might be abandoned, but braver counsels prevailed, the houses were rebuilt, and the work of years was all done over.

The next best thing to staying in Springfield indefinitely is to leave the city behind as slowly as possible. For the accomplishment of this feat the railroad that follows the river bank to the north gives splendid opportunity. "Better wait until eight o'clock and take the Montreal Express; that's a fine train!" a genial adviser said. He was right as to its being a fine train, but he was surely wrong as to its express character. But this is as it should be. Why be in a hurry when visiting the Connecticut Valley?

A choice time for the trip north of Springfield is in May, when the vegetation is reaching maturity there. Hour by hour the foliage becomes less dense, until in upper Vermont the tender buds are just bursting on the trees, the undergrowth is getting a good start, and the birds are singing gleefully as if for joy of what is coming soon. There is nothing like this reversal of nature's spring program to lead to hearty appreciation of the wonder of the annual transformation from snow and ice to balmy air and velvety verdure.

Falls and rapids and dams add to the variety of

the Connecticut north of Springfield. Manufactories innumerable have taken advantage of the water power afforded, notably at Holyoke, where Hadley Falls disturb the river. The present dam is the third constructed there, the first having been built in 1848.

Holyoke is dominated by the hills that rise far above the river, affording wonderful views of the valley at its best, and of the successive terraces by which the land rises from the water to the heights. Geologists tell how these terraces have been the age-long product of the river, scouring a path through the debris left behind by the stream that flowed from the receding front of the glacier to which this valley owes a tremendous debt.

The founder of Mount Holyoke College at South Hadley chose wisely when she decided to build in the heart of this region of terraced hillsides, backed by rugged mountains. The college campus of two hundred acres includes level slopes and uplands, as well as such a real eminence as Prospect Hill, whose wooded heights look down on one of the two lakes which the college girls have all to themselves.

The campus is historic ground, for here, in 1836, was built the first woman's college. A few days after laying the corner-stone, Mary Lyon, the founder, wrote: "I have indeed lived to see the time when a body of gentlemen have ventured to lay the corner stone of a building which will cost fifteen thousand dollars, and will be an institution for the education of females. Surely God hath remembered our state. This will be an era in female education."

Mary Lyon's college has its mountain, just as Smith College, at Northampton, claims one as its peculiar property. From the river both Mount Holyoke and Mount Tom rises in majesty. Both are easy of access, for cars run to the summits. Mount Holyoke affords a wide-spreading panorama of the beautiful valley, and Mount Tom gives opportunity to see a picture of dreamland far below, with the Intervale of the Connecticut—the widening of the valley—as the central feature.

On the top of Mount Tom is a good place to smile at the story of the two Americans who once compared notes when they met on Mont Blanc. One spoke of the view: "Finest thing I have seen in the world, with one exception." "And what is that?" the query came. "The view from Mount Tom," said the loyal son of Massachusetts.

The members of the Edwards family were lovers of the wonderful country about Northampton. Esther, the daughter who became the mother of Aaron Burr, used to wander up the river until she came to the sharp westward sweep that soon becomes an eastward sweep, as if the stream repented of its departure from the straight path. Within the peninsula formed by this ox-bow lies Hadley, some of whose streets reach across the peninsula, having the river for a boundary at both ends. A blind resident on one of these streets has told in "Hitting the Dark Trail," of the joy given to him by this ox-bow:

"I have merely to push my boat on wheels to the head of the street, and then launch it, and I am on one of the most beautiful rivers that ever flowed in a background of meadow and mountains...We at once push our fifteen-foot St. Lawrence River boat, built of cedar, and more treacherous than a canoe, to the further

105

side of the river, and when about fifty feet from the bank, turn her head down stream and float...Onward we glide through the wonderful green meadows, under the great elms that fringe the bank, and the three bridges, until, after two hours, we are back at the foot of my street, only a mile from where we started out, but having covered seven miles of beautiful river to make the distance.''

Years ago there were canoe-men on the river whose spirit was not so innocent as that of this citizen of Hadley. By river as well as by land they watched jealously the movements of the settlers. Deerfield, a few miles north of Hadley, was a special object of their regard. Many times the treachery of the savage was experienced in these towns that were long the frontier of civilization on the upper Connecticut. Finally, in 1704, the town was burned and a company of more than one hundred was marched over snow and ice to Canada. A Memorial Hall in the village shows relics of the Sack of Deerfield, including the door of the one house that successfully resisted, and the record of the adventures of the captives, written by the minister who accompanied them.

Travelers by rail miss a bit of the river from Greenfield to Northfield, for the stream makes a right angled turn to the west, and the railroad is the hypothenuse of the triangle. But they are well repaid for the brief privation by the stretch of rolling green fields through which they are taken. The country, with its background of swelling, wooded slopes makes special appeal as the train approaches Mount Hermon.

Before reaching Northfield, the river is seen once more, and its charms seem to have increased in the interval to such an extent that the last miles in Massachusetts are, if possible, the best in the fifty-mile stretch across the state. The knobs and ridges of East Northfield, on the east side of the river, speak in praise of the founder of the Northfield Seminary, the last of the eight or nine educational institutions of national and even world-wide fame that have been crowded within forty miles along or close to the Connecticut.

For a portion of the way between Brattleboro, Vermont, and Northfield, the river widens between the bordering hills. This was the country to which Rudyard Kipling came for a season, rejoicing in its waters and its woodlands. At Brattleboro he invited his friends to his country place, "The Naulahka," and prepared some of his matchless books, notably "Captains Courageous." Beetling cliffs, rounded terraces, and shady nooks greeted his eyes wherever he turned, and some of these must have influenced his thought.

The site later occupied by Brattleboro was marked indelibly in the memory of the victims of the Sack of Deerfield, for where West River empties into the Connecticut they left the land where they had made a toilsome journey and took to the frozen river on snowshoes and in dog sledges which the Indians had left at this point on their way south.

In later years peace-loving Indians sought Fort Dummer, founded in 1725 where later William Brattle laid out the town that was to be a center of conflict in the contest between New Hampshire and New York to possess the territory on the west side of the river. There Governor Banning Wentworth of New Hampshire had made his grants, claiming as that

107

state's western boundary a line twenty miles east of the Hudson River.

Bennington, some distance over the hills to the west of Brattleboro, was another storm center. Though named for Governor Wentworth, who made grants to settlers there, its residents later wished to unit the many grants west of the Connecticut, which ultimately extended far up toward the Canada line. The Hanover College party at Dartmouth, on the contrary, schemed for a New Connecticut, whose capital was to be in the neighborhood of the college, and whose territory was to be made up of grants on both sides of the river. In the meantime conflicting court decisions and the activity of Ethan Allen's Green Mountain Boys, organized for the purpose of resisting attempts to dispossess the dwellers on the west of the Connecticut by officers from New York, added to the excitement of the Valley, until the Revolution brought a temporary cessation of hostilities.

Twenty miles above Brattleboro gorge busy Bellows Falls has its seat beside another gorge. There a canal with eight locks was constructed early in the nineteenth century. This was one of a series of canals at intervals between Holyoke, Massachusetts, and White River, Vermont, built to facilitate navigation to a point more than two hundred miles above Hartford. Until the railroad made water transportation unnecessary the Connecticut was a busy stream, thanks to these ingenious canals. Ruined locks and half-choked channels speak eloquently of those picturesque days.

After leaving Bellows Falls, with its mysterious-looking covered bridge, the railroad crosses into New Hampshire and from the east side follows the windings of the river until it re-enters Vermont below a second covered bridge that makes those who see it eager to stand within its portals and look between its cracks down to towering Mount Ascutney.

Bountifully endowed by nature, Windsor has also the distinction of being the birthplace of Vermont. In 1777, at the consitutional convention there, the government was organized by the towns west of the river, as well as sixteen towns east of the river. Hanover and the Dartmouth College authorities agreed to the new arrangement. Yet it was five years before New Hampshire's boundaries were declared to extend as far as the west bank of the river.

Dartmouth College, from its sightly height on the east bank, looks off to the hills and mountains of New Hampshire, and down on the river where students are fond of rowing under the pine grove that crowds close to the water. Sometimes as they rest in the dense shade they talk of John Ledyard, the student who, in 1773, made a canoe from a pine tree and descended the Connecticut to Hartford, thus giving a prophecy of the restless career during which he influenced Thomas Jefferson to send Lewis and Clark to the Northwest and made him successively a partner of John Paul Jones and a pioneer fur trader of the west.

This fascinating stretch of river seems to have had a fashion of developing pioneers in transportation. A few miles north, in 1792-1793, between Fairlee, Vermont and Orford, New Hampshire, Samuel Morey tested a steamboat built by himself, which ran so successfully against the current that he took it down the river for more ambitious trials. Later he constructed another and larger boat, and consulted with

Robert Fulton and John Fitch. The model of the engine of "the first American boat propelled by paddle-wheels" is preserved with great pride in Fairlee, whose people never weary of talking of the jovial farmer-inventor who gave fame to their stretch of river, flowing serenely through the alluvial valley.

At Fairlee the traveler rejoices as he looks over the river into New Hampshire. In Orford the houses cluster amid the trees about the white spire of the village church. Beyond rise the successive ridges of rounded summits. The eye lingers lovingly on a sugar-loaf peak mounting in superb dignity above irregular slopes.

To many the best of the river is still beyond. Though the railroad leaves it, the highway follows its banks as it stretches away to the northeast, forming the boundary that rapidly brings New Hampshire almost to a point, rounding more ox-bow bends, crossing tributary streams innumerable, leading past the distant White Mountains and their northern outposts, and on to the first of the series of lakes where the stream has its source, Connecticut Lake, more than sixteen hundred feet above the sea. From this point there is a fine opportunity to scramble a few miles through wild, wooded territory to Second and Third Lakes, and finally Fourth Lake, the ultimate source of the Connecticut, just below the Canadian boundary, and more than twenty-five hundred feet above sea level. Hereabouts was the country so far removed from civilization that in 1829 the settlers organized themselves as "The United Inhabitants of the Indian Stream Territory," taking the name from the western tributary of the Connecticut. This strangest of all transient governments that from time to time have been set up within the boundaries of the United States declared itself independent both of this country and of Great Britain. After five years, however, the territory melted away.

But many travelers must bid a regretful farewell to the winding stream either at Wells River or at St. Johnsbury, turning toward Burlington and Lake Champlain. If their chosen route is from St. Johnsbury, they have a heartening climb over the Green Mountains, past Joe's Pond, up Walden Ridge and by Caspian Lake. The scenery is rugged, and there is often a two per cent grade. If the journey lakeward is begun at Wells River Junction, the back is turned on the White Mountains, and the attention is riveted by winding Wells River, foaming over the rocks for a mile or two before it enters the Connecticut. Farther on it sometimes rushes fiercely, then flows quietly. But how it turns and twists! And how the railroad builders must have blessed it as they had to make frequent crossings from side to side! Yet probably their thankfulness exceeded their displeasure, for the troublesome stream opened a satisfactory way through the mountains.

Above the recalcitrant river rise the hills, where the rocks are scattered on the sides as if thrown out from a great pepper box. Below are valleys where the glacier was generous in dealing out the supply of bowlders.

Later the road pushes its way among the granite-crowned ridges of the Green Mountains. Some, for variety, have precipitous granite sides and green summits.

The descent toward Montpelier is high above the

Winooski River, which here is turbid enough, though at Burlington it enters the lake very quietly.

But the passage of the traveler to Burlington is not so easy. He has yet to change cars two or three times. To ride in four trains between Wells River and Lake Champlain—less than one hundred miles—would be trying, but for the opportunity the waits afford to hark back to the pilgrimage up the wonderful Connecticut, the Beautiful River.

CHAPTER XIII

ROUND ABOUT NEW YORK CITY

B UT think of the time you will lose!" said a hurrying business man, who goes daily from his New
Jersey home to his office in New York, to a visitor who ventured to suggest that he preferred to cross
the Hudson by ferry rather than by one of the marvelous tunnels far down in the rock under the stream.

Yet the visitor was glad to exchange a bit of time
for twenty minutes in one of the commodious ferry
boats that ply like shuttles from shore to shore, weaving
in and out among the barges from the Erie Canal,
scows bound for the outer harbor, and boats that carry
a dozen freight cars loaded, perhaps, with provisions
for the great city; skilfully avoiding an important-
looking tug; slowing up to permit a great ocean steamer
to pass on its way; or whistling shrill warning to a
tramp steamer whose staring red plates tell of long
months of service where wind and wave forget that
there is such a thing as moderation.

The busy river is so crowded with attractions that
the eyes are tempted to stray from the panorama on
shore, where buildings tall and buildings yet more tall
form a marvelous sky line that to most people never
loses its novelty. Miles long, from the Battery far
beyond Forty-Second Street, it notches the eastern
heavens with domes and turrets and pinnacles as well
as with roofs that are frankly, prosaically plain. It
is easy to pick out some of the landmarks, like the

Hudson Terminal, the Woolworth Building, or the Metropolitan Building. But who wants to separate into its elements a picture that would be the despair of an Arabian Nights dreamer or a Monte Christo on his travels?

And who would be so foolish as to declare that there is any best season to behold the picture in all its magnificence? Is there a time when the vision of New York from a Hudson River ferryboat is not tremendously impressive? When the sunbeams turn into jewels the million windows of the busy hives of industry; when the dawning light of a new day discloses the ranks of masonry in ghostly array; when the air is full of swirling snow that, like a half-revealing curtain, makes closer inspection seem desirable; when the mist forms a veil between the observer and the towers of steel; when, at evening, the beacon lights begin to glow from roof to foundation—then is the choice time to see the stately panorama that beckons the traveler on his approach to New York City and lingers in his memory when for years, perhaps, he has been far from the metropolis.

The ferryboat offers only a beginning of the trip that should be taken by water, entirely around Manhattan Island—down past tooth-like piers that reach out into the river from Seventieth Street to the Battery; past Castle Garden, for many years the landing place for the immigrants from Europe; on through the Narrows to Bedloe's Island with its blinking Statue of liberty, and to Ellis Island, gateway today for the hordes who seek the land of liberty; back to the East River, where, on the right, Brooklyn invites the traveler to visit the streets and parks of a city as large as

THE TIP OF MANHATTAN ISLAND
Castle Garden and Battery Park in the Foreground

ST. PAUL'S CHAPEL, NEW YORK CITY
Erected 1764

Philadelphia, though now it has united its destinies with those of the giant that reached out from its lair on Manhattan and appropriated everything within reach, except regions protected from its encroachments by state lines.

Just ahead looms the stately Brooklyn Bridge, the original East River suspension bridge, which stretches from shore to shore one hundred and thirty-five feet above the water. This bridge a great engineer has called "one of the most beautiful structures in the world." The stately curve formed by the slender supporting cables, the massive, majestic stone towers, the web of steel between the towers, the graceful road-way, "springing from pier to pier and sloping on each side to earth," combine to make an artistic dream that is the admiration of the beholder as it has been the despair of the builders of later bridges across the river. Manhattan Bridge, with its impressive proportions, Williamsburg Bridge, the world's greatest suspension bridge, and Queensboro Bridge, a marvel of cantilever construction, all must bow to the older structure.

Queensboro Bridge, farthest north of the four, crosses high above Blackwell's Island, refuge of New York's petty criminals, which—to those who can see it from the air—looks like the hull of a great ocean greyhound.

Beyond Blackwell's Island is infamous Hell Gate, where treacherous reefs and violent currents due to the conflicting tides that come from the Narrows and from Long Island Sound, were the dread of navigators until the reefs were removed after gigantic preparations that involved the blasting of tunnels, the building of a coffer dam, and the planting of explosives in thousands

115

of holes skilfully prepared for their reception. Thus passage through the channel was made comparatively safe, as passage above the channel has been made easy by the construction of the great Hell Gate Bridge used by the through trains between Washington and Boston.

The circuit of Manhattan is completed by the passage, west of Ward's Island and Randall's Island, into Harlem River, whose waters are crossed successively by the Viaduct, nearly one mile long, High Bridge, which carries Croton Aqueduct over the Harlem, and Washington Bridge, which is as high as Brooklyn Bridge.

More than thirty miles of water front! But when the circuit of Manhattan has been completed, but twenty-two of the three hundred and twenty-six square miles of Greater New York have been circumscribed. Yet these twenty-two square miles contain the most historic and picturesque portion of the city.

Those who enter New York by the Hudson and Manhattan tunnels from Jersey City find themselves at once in the heart of the busy metropolis, only a short walk from Battery Park, at the southern end of the island. There Washington used to walk, and there idlers and sightseers still stroll along the pavements or lounge on the benches in the shadow of the first of the city's skyscrapers.

Other haunts of Washington are near. At the corner of Fulton Street venerable St. Paul's Chapel bids defiance to the traffic of the busy adjacent streets and looks up serenely at the tall buildings whose bulk is a startlingly picturesque background for its steeple. The old churchyard with its crumbling stones and the

116

mellowed walls of the structure that saw the pomp of colonial days seem like a bit of old London. Within doors that look out on the graves of worthies of long ago Washington frequently passed, notably for his first inauguration, when he sought the chapel to ask God's blessing on the infant country over whose destiny he had been called to preside.

In the days of the first President St. Paul's was surrounded by open spaces, but now the churchyard— an oasis of green in a wilderness of brick and steel and granite—is the refuge of women from the tenements, of old men who live in the past, of young people to whom ten years seem an age, while the days of the beginnings of the chapel are prehistoric. On almost any bright day a woman may be seen sitting on a flat tomb, eyes now bent on her knitting, again lifted to her little charges as they toddle along the graves. At noon stenographers, with lunch and fancy-work, spend a half hour within the protecting shadow of the chapel. And always there are passing through the portico the curious, the careless and the patriotic who go to the pew where Washington worshipped or stand in the vestibule before the statue of General Montgomery, the hero of Quebec.

Within easy walking distance of St. Paul's Chapel is the steeple of historic Trinity Church, which long since gave up the struggle with the towering buildings of the Wall Street section. These have risen where, in 1644, on "Monday, being the 4th of April," every burgher was warned to repair with tools to aid in constructing a fence "beginning at the Great Bouwery and extending to Emannuel's plantation." This fence proved such a protection against Indians and such a help in preventing cattle from straying that, in 1653, it was determined to build on the same site a palisade for the further protection of the city. The palisade was 340 feet long, and its cost was $1300.

The palisade of 1653 gave the name to Wall Street, even as a sharp practitioner of the street of those days has found some successors who bring discredit to a district which others have endeavored to keep beyond reproach. The story is told that the street before the wall or palisade, when first projected, was to be one hundred feet wide. The purchaser of a long strip of ground eighty feet deep, adjoining the site of the proposed street, managed to limit the width of the new thoroughfare to thirty-six feet, and the sixty-four feet thus stolen from the public made his lots both deep and valuable!

The distance is short to City Hall Park, the site of the beautiful classic City Hall, whose design won a prize of three hundred and fifty dollars, while the architect received six dollars a day for his services! The builders thought they were making a daring prophecy of the city's future when they erected such a mammoth structure. They did not dream, when they made the north wall of brownstone, because it would not be seen, that this wall would be observed by as many as the south facade. They would have been equally amazed if they had been told that their venture a whole mile away from the Battery, would leave the building many miles from the heart of the city of the early years of the twentieth century, or that the structure that seemed to be so magnificent would some day have as neighbors a twelve-million-dollar County Court House, a six-million-dollar Hall of Records, and a fifteen-million-dollar Municipal Building, to say nothing of the towering Woolworth Building, fifty-five stories high.

"Take the subway if you wish to go to Forty-Second Street," a well-meaning passenger said to a visitor who was bound north from City Hall Square. He could not understand why any thinking man should wish to take half an hour to ride through the congested streets when he could take the subway and be at his destination before he had a good chance to become accustomed to the transition from the hubbub of the upper world with its ever changing pictures to the bright lights and the utter absence of color of the dungeon.

The subway is a good thing—when it is necessary to take it. But the Broadway car plows its way through scenes varied and appealing. It passes within reach of the Washington Arch, whose classic columns rise between picturesque Greenwich Village on the west, and the streets that lead to the teeming East Side tenement district. It passes Union Square, with its statues of Washington and Lafayette and Lincoln, as well as Madison Square, where statues of famous men are neighbors of idlers who loll on the benches while the clock in Metropolitan Tower chimes many quarter hours. It crosses the path of the noonday throng of garment-workers who crowd Fifth Avenue for some distance north of Nineteenth Street, and so help to bring down the rents of the buildings that abut on their chosen line of march; it passes the Flatiron Building, which to many is the typical office building of the metropolis; it gives a fleeting glimpse of the many-columned portico of the great Pennsylvania Station, before which a noted English writer stood in wonder, while he declared that in Europe the station would be worthy to be a cathedral. When that man saw the Grand Central Terminal, he was speechless: the idea that one city could have two such structures was to him amazing.

It is not enough to see the sights of Broadway by daylight; the street should be visited at night, when the bright lights make it the famous "Great White Way." Then the theater district, on both sides of Longacre Square from Forty-Second to Fiftieth Street, is thronged with amusement-seekers. While they are on the way to their chosen places of recreation, motor buses on the side streets are taking toll from those who would go to Coney Island. And when, near midnight, the theater-goers are on the street once more, drivers of other buses tell of the charms of Chinatown, giving veiled hints of something forbidden. But those who go in company of the loud-mouthed guardians of the Chinatown bus soon learn that they have set out on a very circumspect tour, after all.

The most democratic motor bus of all threads Fifth Avenue. Let no one who has not looked down from a seat on deck, as he has ridden from Forty-Second Street to Washington Heights, think that he has seen Manhattan. For he will pass the Public Library, with its broad, hospitable entrance; he will get a glimpse of Central Park; he will pass over the famous Riverside Drive, one of the most famous of the world's boulevards, with spacious apartment houses and comfortable homes on the east, while on the west, far below, the Hudson moves onward to the sea. The roadway twists and turns, passing close to the slowly growing Cathedral of St. John the Divine, begun in 1892, to be

120

completed after many more decades; the new Columbia University; the tomb of Grant, where all Americans delight to go, even if they do differ greatly as to the architectural pretensions of the structure; and, finally, the Morris-Jumel Mansion, built by Robert Morris in 1766, where Washington was a guest in 1776.

But not even yet is the limit of Manhattan reached. At the extreme end of the island Van Cortlandt Park with its eleven hundred acres invites the stranger to wander along its picturesque roadways until he comes to the Van Cortlandt Mansion, built in 1748 by Frederick Van Cortlandt. Here, in 1783, Washington was entertained.

And beyond the Park and across the Harlem River, is the Bronx, a section of Greater New York that is as large as Detroit.

CHAPTER XIV

THE HUDSON HIGHLANDS PARADISE

IN 1877 a lad of fifteen began work as an office boy in lower New York City. While he himself had many opportunities to go here and there for recreation, his heart was touched as he saw the boys and girls of the tenements whose playground was the street, whose sky was clouded by smoke and fog, whose outlook on life was as hopeless as their surroundings. Even then he determined that some day he would do his best to change these trying conditions.

Years passed. The office boy, whose name was George W. Perkins, became a busy man, a leader in politics, in business, in civic affairs. Then, one day in 1900, sounded a clarion call to unpaid service of a sort that many men would have declined. It came by the prosaic long distance telephone. "Theodore Roosevelt speaking," was the introduction. The Governor of New York then said to him, "I am appointing a commission to save the Palisades, and have named you as president." To the reply that it would be necessary to think over the matter, in view of many engagements, Governor Roosevelt made decisive answer, "I did not call you up to ask you *whether* you would accept the appointment; I called you up to tell you that you *are* the president of the Commissioners of the Palisades Interstate Park."

It was enough. Mr. Perkins saw his opportunity. Now he could do something for the poor of New York

City; incidentally, also, for those who could travel where they would in search of the picturesque. He knew the Palisades. He had seen them from the river; he had driven along the heights; he had climbed the innumerable trails that lead up from the water front to the cliffs from three hundred to five hundred feet high. The knowledge gained during these jaunts, and the vision of opportunity set before him by Roosevelt led him to write:

"Who has not stood in awe at the wonderful lava-rock Palisades extending on the west bank of the Hudson River from opposite One Hundred and Thirtieth Street, New York, to a point opposite Hastings? The old Dutch voyagers called the Palisades near Hook Mountain 'Verdrietegh Hook,' meaning 'Grievous Point.' It was well named, for it has been for many years a grievous point whether the trap rock quarrying interests should chip this formation to sell it by the yard, or whether the Palisades should be preserved as a great park. This 'point' brought into existence the Commissioners of the Palisades Interstate Park, appointed by the Governors of New York and New Jersey, who were intrusted with the purchase, location and administration of what is now a twelve-mile parkway. The crushed stone chipped from these famous headlands was used considerably in the building of the tenements where, deprived of the freedom of outdoors, the people were in special need of a breathing space to lift their crushed souls from the shattering influence of the throbbing city to the exalted contact of the out-of-doors."

Enthusiastically the members of the two commissions set to work to put the sheltering arms of the state about the region of unparalleled grandeur and beauty. The beginning of the work of conservation was characteristic. Instead of spending in investigations the initial appropriation made, the entire sum was paid to the owner for an option on a large quarry which was rapidly wrecking one of the towering cliffs. J. Pierpont Morgan supplied the funds to complete the purchase. An appeal was made for further appropriations to purchase a twelve-mile strip along the Hudson's shore from near Fort Lee to a point opposite Yonkers. The larger part of this section is in New Jersey, but the northern portion is in New York.

The area thus secured for the people has been developed, not by attempts to improve on nature, but by the construction of drives and trails. There is a drive along the summit which affords surprising glimpses of the river and breath-taking vistas across into New York. A beginning has been made of the Henry Hudson Drive on the water front. Trails innumerable have been constructed up and along the cliff, disclosing the secrets of hidden nooks and leaping waterfalls and giving opportunities for rock-climbing such as the uninitiated would expect to find only in the wilds far from the city.

To think that these privileges are available within ten minutes of upper Broadway—for a ten-cent fare on the ferry!

That the swarming multitudes of New York City might have every chance for wholesome recreation, the commission arranged to utilize the land on the heights as well as on the shore beneath the towering cliffs. Artificial plateaus for picnic parties were constructed of stone from the New York subways. Of the waste

124

screenings from stone crushers a thousand-foot bathing beach was made at a point opposite One Hundred and Fifty-Eighth Street. A bath house which can be used by thousands at one time was built from waste rock and from lumber cut farther north in the Hudson Highlands, on Interstate Park land. Pavilions were placed on the heights, for the use of picnickers and followers of the romantic trails carved into the cliffs, "paths which plunged into the pristine splendor of the woods and rockland," to quote Mr. Perkins. There are boat basins where row boats and motor boats find shelter, one of these being at Alpine, less than two miles from the beginning of the Park. Those who land at this point find themselves at the foot of the old wagon road that makes perilous and picturesque descent down the Palisades from Closter, several miles in the interior, to the house of wood and stone occupied as headquarters by Cornwallis during the Revolution, but now used by the park police.

In fulfilment of the purpose to make this a great playground for the million, camps have been built where there is abundant provision for comfort and health, and camping sites are available at a nominal rental. In fact, everything except scenery, and pleasure, and health are nominal in the Palisades Interstate Park. There are no concessions for the money-maker; everything is for the people. "My idea of a public park is to have it do, on a non-commercial basis, all the finer things which are to be found in other recreation centers," one of the park-builders has said.

From the beginning those who have followed the work of the two state commissions have marveled. At the time of dedication Governor Fort of New Jersey asked if it was possible that so valuable a piece of property was ever purchased at such a reasonable price.

Not long after Governor Fort gave expression to his surprise at what has been accomplished, something more wonderful still came to pass. In 1910 the crowded condition of New York's Sing Sing Prison led to the purchase of land for a prison camp and, ultimately, a penitentiary, in the shadow of Bear Mountain, on the west bank of the Hudson, between West Point and Tompkins Cove. But the thought that one of the finest locations in the Hudson Highlands was to be taken from the people for such use led to vigorous protests from the citizens of Highland Falls, several miles north of the proposed site. Public-spirited residents of New York joined them in the protest, insisting that it would be a crime to devote to such use a spot that looked over the river to Anthony's Nose, the southern entrance to the Highlands; down the river to Iona Island and Dunderberg Mountain, with Stony Point beyond; and up to the more northerly heights, where Sugar Loaf Hill dominates the horizon.

The protest was effective. The Legislature turned over the new prison site to the Commission of the Interstate Park, with the request that they develop it as they had developed the Palisades. Soon there was a celebration of the transfer of the plateau at the base of Bear Mountain. During the exercises W. Averill Harriman, a member of the Commission, said that it was his privilege to be the agent of his mother, Mrs. E. H. Harriman, in carrying out the dream of his father to give to the people a large portion of the family Arden Estate, adjoining the Bear Mountain region. Ten

126

EL CAPITAN, NEAR FOREST VIEW, IN THE PALISADES

BEAR MOUNTAIN LANDING ON THE HUDSON

thousand acres of virgin forest and one million dollars were included in the gift.

Again Mr. Perkins had a vision, and once more he imparted his enthusiasm to his fellows on the Commission. The one-million-dollar fund was multiplied by five, through other gifts and by means of a state bond issue. Other tracts were bought, until the total holdings of the Commission, in New Jersey and New York, were increased to more than forty thousand acres, the larger part of these being in the Harriman Park Area, reaching back for seventeen miles from the Hudson, almost to Tuxedo and the Ramapo Hills, to the hidden valley in the wilds where the Erie Railroad creeps in on New York City.

Here was a region of rugged hills and dimpling valleys, of dense forests and tree-clad mountains, of limpid lakes and leaping, shaded brooks to which there was access only by primitive roads and paths, except through the Ramapo Valley. One of the best-built roads in the country—the "Road of Seven Lakes"— was taken by a winding route far back into the interior. Other roads were added to the system. Trails were laid out, the natural beauty of lakes and streams was enhanced by dams, and rustic camps were placed in advantageous locations far from the Bear Mountain landing. These camps were built of timber cut wisely in the park and prepared in the Commission's own sawmills. They were then rented to various organizations which would help carry out the purpose of the park, and for the nominal annual sum of fiften per cent of the cost of building.

At Bear Mountain an inn of logs was built. It looks like a Swiss chalet, and it has an outlook both up and

127

down the river that a Swiss chalet might envy. All around are the green mountains. The dining room looks across to Anthony's Nose, on whose towering summit beacons were lit during the Revolution, that these might be seen from another height above West Point and passed on to the north.

Bear Mountain Inn is a novelty. There are no accomodations for lodgers, but there is ample provision for the needs of the thousands who seek its portals nearly every day during the entire summer. It has its own ice plant, bottling establishment, and bakery; in fact it has everything that can be thought of, and some things that would not occur to anyone but a seasoned hotel man.

Close to the inn is the dancing pavilion, located within a short distance of the site of the battle fought by the British for the possession of Fort Montgomery, whose earthworks may still be traced just across Popolopen Creek. Also near at hand is Hessian Lake, where rowboats are supplied free, yet in such a manner that the people pay the expense of the service. The deposit of twenty-five cents made for the use of a boat is handed back when the craft is returned within half an hour. Thus only those pay who are able to pay.

The same principle regulates other charges in the park. There is automobile service to four distinct zones, from ten miles to forty miles. For this the charge is small, yet it is sufficient to make possible the transportation of the poor from New York City to the Bear Mountain dock, forty-five miles, then to the chosen camp deep within the park, from five to

128

seventeen miles, and finally back to New York City, for a merely nominal charge.

In like manner any profits made from those able to pay more for food were sufficient to make possible the supply of twenty-one balanced meals a week, sent warm by automobile from the inn to boys and girls in the camps at a charge that seems ridiculously small. Every effort was made to hold to a minimum any change in these figures made necessary by increasing cost.

Transportation by the Hudson River Day Line is cheap, but it is not cheap enough to suit the Commissioners. So an arrangement was made for a steamer controlled by themselves which at first took passengers from Jersey City to the park and return for fifty cents!

For the accommodation of the landing passengers, a two-hundred-foot dock was built. Doubters said that it would be one hundred years before the accommodation thus provided would be taxed. This prophecy seemed to be proven true when, on the first trip to Bear Mountain after the opening of Harriman Park, but two people took passage. On the first holiday only sixty-five people entered the park. During the first summer the largest crowd on one day was seven hundred people.

The faith of the dock builders has been justified. The fame of the park has grown until more than a million and a half visitors come to it each year. Sometimes one, two, or even three heavily laden steamers may be seen waiting their turn to land.

It is remarkable that not one-third of the merrymakers who throng to the park know what riches are waiting for them. "It is safe to say that at least a million of those who come here in the course of the season have no idea that there is anything to the park back of the inn, the plateau, the lake, and Bear Mountain," said Captain Gee, of the Park Police, the author's companion on a trip over forty miles of the reservation's most interesting roads and trails.

The pride of the guardians of the Highland recreation area is the Seven Lakes Drive, which begins its winding course by skirting Bear Mountain, far above the river as it reaches southeast toward Peekskill. A turn discloses the bowl-like Doodletown Valley, a vision of rare beauty, between West Mountain on one side and Dunderberg Mountain and the Timp on the other. Doodleberg village nestles opposite. Both village and valley, it is said, commemorate the march of the British troops through the region on the way from Stony Point to Fort Montgomery. As they passed through the valley, in derision the band played Yankee Doodle. Hence the name Doodleberg!

A part of the modern drive was built on the site of the primitive road traversed by the British that day. On the right, by Queensboro Lake, a portion of the old road is quite plain, and stretches away through the forest.

Off to the left are the reminders of Queensboro Furnace, where were forged the great links of the chain stretched across the Hudson to Anthony's Nose, as well as from West Point to Constitution Island, in the effort to hamper British advance up the river.

Queensboro Brook, tumbling over the rocks or pausing in deep pools, tells of the trout and the bass that lurk within its waters. Better fishing ground is Cedar Lake, which has been formed by damming a valley and uniting two ponds. Its six hundred acres are varied by several boggy floating islands, as well as by others

130

that are on rock foundations. Already the road has risen more than eleven hundred feet above the river to the watershed between the Hudson and the Ramapo Valley. On this height it would be easy to imagine that the scene is in the heart of Washington or Oregon; in fact, visitors from the Pacific Coast were heard to remark at this point, "At last we have seen something that makes us think of home."

Beyond Cedar Lake is the Kamehwauke chain of lakes, on whose long reaches provision is made in sixteen camps for thousands of New Jersey and New York Boy Scouts. There they can fish and row to their heart's content. In the biggest of the lakes is a group of islands where the Sea Scouts learn the lore of the sailor and gain experience that enables the best of them to go back to New York in big sea-going rowboats, camping at night on the shore. Those who do not go in for sea scouting are guided as they track through the forests, learn the use of the compass in the depths of the woods, study wild life by the aid of manuals prepared under state authority, and gain knowledge of the plants and the trees of the wild.

These campers in the wilderness like to go to Cranberry Hill, where the Southfield back road looks off into the Ramapo Valley, and over to Tuxedo. They pause among the masses of rock by the side of the road, above it, or down below. They look with delight at the cascades that dash down the mountain side, like that of Carr Pond Creek, (outlet of Lake Stahahe), which they can see so plainly from the highway bridge. With laughing music the waters toss from rock to rock, beneath the bending hemlocks and birches, by the side

131

of ferns of half a dozen varieties that grow, it may be within a square yard.

On the edge of the Ramapo Valley is the enclosure for native deer and for elk from Yellowstone Park, an enclosure so large that the animals can hardly feel that they are imprisoned.

Then comes the leafy drive through the Harriman Estate, and down to Greenwood Furnace, at the foot of Ramapo Mountain—another relic of Revolutionary days. Farther along are Echo Lake, one of the most beautiful bodies of water in the park, surrounded by spruce-covered heights, and Arden Valley Falls, remarkable for the precipitous descent of a large volume of water.

Summit Lake Camp for members of the Young Women's Christian Association, by isolated Summit Lake, nine hundred feet above the river, may be approached by an automobile road from Central Valley, New York, or by the Erie railroad. Other camps for young women are on the Seven Lakes, which have been made accessible by the road over Long Mountain. This new road, a short cut back to the highway that leads along the Doodletown Valley and back to Bear Mountain, affords one of the most striking prospects in the park, toward Quannacut, the Rainbow Camp for schoolgirls, then over the valley to Little Rock Mountain beyond.

Once, when Mr. Perkins was asked if it had paid to devote the efforts of so many years to developing this Paradise for the People, he replied, with deep feeling:

"If you could only see the sparkle in the sad eyes of the orphan, or the smile that plays around the drooped mouth of some little child who has been deprived of the normal use of his limbs; if you could see the warmth which comes into the heart of the little child who for the first time disports in those heavenly fields or feel the stir of imagination and exaltation which comes to the tired working girl as she sits restfully beneath a tree enjoying her respite from dear and deadly monotony of the ship! Your State is safer in the hands of children whose health is being protected, whose vision is not distorted, and who look back at what was done for them under the auspices of the State with satisfaction and appreciation.''

CHAPTER XV

IN RIP VAN WINKLE'S CATSKILLS

D O you suppose we could make a circuit of the Catskill Mountains in a day?" was the query of the guide of an automobile party who seemed to think that the success of the expedition depended on covering ground in as short a time as possible.

"Yes, I suppose you could," was the pitying reply. "The roads are rather well arranged for your purpose, and most of them are good. Yet I doubt if you could gain the consent of your party to carry out your plan; you would be committing a crime against Nature."

The Catskills are compact; they are a miniature, pocket edition of the best American mountains, set down at the doorway of the country's greatest city, within easy reach of more people than any other outstanding feature of the country's scenery. But both compactness and ease of access are arguments for leisurely appreciation rather than hasty sight-seeing.

The front door of the Catskills—the Hudson River —provides appetizing first glimpses of the mountains for twenty-five miles south of Athens. Back beyond the smiling valley that borders the river rise successive green ridges. In places the nearest ridge lifts leisurely in easy terraces. Looking from the circumscribed car windows of a West Shore train, the observer is apt to think, "Surely that will be the last terrace." But

A WINDING ROAD IN ESOPUS VALLEY, CATSKILL MOUNTAINS

others follow in rapid succession, until the horizon is bounded by a long series of graceful contours.

If the traveler has time it will be to his advantage to leave the train at West Athens, ride—or better, walk—the two miles to Athens, then take the ferry across the Hudson. At ebb tide this crossing gives an especially advantageous view of distant glory, for it is necessary to drop down stream before making for the landing. And every moment of the little journey is a season of such delight that it is difficult to resist the temptation to repeat the crossing many times.

From Hudson the eyes travel swiftly across to Kaaterskill, near the border of the Catskill Park, the reservation in which New York State owns more than one hundred thousand of the nearly six hundred thousand acres included in this heart of the Catskills. Kaaterskill is close to the spot from which Natty Bumpo in The Pioneers said he could see "all creation."

Within a short distance of Kaaterskill, and less than two miles apart, are two of the typical waterfalls of the Catskills, Haines Falls and Kaaterskill Falls, plunging from precipices where trees crowd down close to the water's edge.

An enticing railroad wanders from Kaaterskill within call of some of the finest bits of the Catskills—mountains that reach on high up to four thousand feet, cloves or passes that divide the mountain ridges and invite pedestrians who like to scramble, creek valleys, like the Stony Clove Creek and Esopus Creek, and, finally, the great Ashokan Reservoir, the lake which New York City constructed for its water supply.

Incidentally, the guide to Ashokan can present a wonderful array of figures—nearly thirteen square miles of area, forty miles of shore line, occupying the site of seven villages, displacing sixty-four miles of highways, and eleven miles of railroad.

But far more interesting is the fact that from the shore of the lake, and from the causeway that divides it into two parts, may be seen some of the choicest prospects in the Catskill area. From west to north the panorama includes High Point, Hanover, Cornell and Wittenberg, and even a bit of Slide Mountain, whose 4,204 feet make it king of the Catskills.

The terminus of the Ulster and Delaware Railroad is Kingston, which is also the starting-point on one of the choicest scenic highways in the East, the historic route through the valley of the Rondout and the Neversink, to Port Jervis. From the days of the Dutch colonists to the weary years when Washington guarded this Western Border, in the attempt to frustrate the designs of the British to cut off New England from the South, this was a path of empire.

A section of the route to the north of beautiful Mohawk Lake and dreamy Minnewaska, was long called The Old Mine Road, because of an expedition conducted—it is surmised by some historian—by the Dutch West India Company, in the belief that great mineral wealth existed in the Minisink region. Because control of the country had passed from the Dutch to the English, great secrecy was observed in this adventure. It has been conjectured that the tunnel in Shawangunk Mountain that has mystified visitors to charming Ellenville is a relic of this search for treasure. This tunnel enters the solid rock of the mountain for a distance of more than five hundred feet. It is six feet high and four feet wide, and has two side tunnels each about fifty feet long. How the vast work was done, so far from the source of supplies, and without the knowledge of those who would have told of it even if they had not endeavored to prevent it, is a puzzle that adds to the pleasure of days spent in this southern portion of the Catskill country.

To the east of Ellenville, and beyond Minnewaska, is the height above the Hudson chosen long ago by John Burroughs as the site for his retreat, Slabsides. There he wrote his name deep on the Catskill country in which he was born, and where he spent most of his days. The old farmhouse at Roxbury, in the Western Catskills, that sheltered him as a boy was almost in the shadow of Old Clump Mountain. On the shoulder of the mountain, or along the banks of the Pepacton, eastern branch of the Delaware, he delighted to wander. And to this vicinity he went back in his old age, rebuilding an old farmhouse half a mile from his birthplace, and christening it Woodchuck Lodge.

The Lodge was chosen because of the view across the sloping meadows, to the wooded slopes that rise swiftly and gracefully in rounded beauty.

Above the Lodge the prospect is yet more glorious: Double Top and Mount Graham lift themselves above the valley and look away to Grand Gorge on Bear Kill and Mount Utsayantha, which is remarkable not only for the view of the slopes from the surrounding valleys, but as well for the sweeping vistas, from the summit, of well-tilled fields and densely wooded intervales.

CHAPTER XVI

ALONG EASTERN NEW YORK BY WATER

MORE than three hundred years ago the first explorers ventured on the mysteries of Eastern New York's majestic series of north and south waterways and marvelled at their sublime beauty. In 1609 Hudson ascended the river that bears his name, and in the same year Champlain penetrated far toward the source of the Hudson where his wondering eyes beheld the shores and islands of the lake that is his enduring monument. They followed hordes of Indians to whom the river and the lakes had long been the favorite route from the bay to the St. Lawrence, and they have been followed through the centuries by other Indians, by rival claimants to the fair lands of the red men, and by pioneers and travelers unnumbered.

In the early days the route was a liability as well as an asset to the hardy settlers who fringed the water courses; access to them was as easy for their enemies as for their friends. But the liability almost disappeared during the Revolution when the British failed in their efforts to divide the colonies by gaining possession of the river and lakes. The attempt was renewed, in part, during the War of 1812, but it was even less successful than before.

Now for more than a century New York State has been able to realize without hindrance on the assets. The keen business man has been apt to define these assets in commercial terms, but those who prefer to talk of the scenic glories of the three-hundred-mile stretch are becoming more numerous each year. Of the millions who annually take passage on steamers that follow where Hudson and Champlain blazed the way, multitudes for the first time see this ancient route of the Indian, and go home under the spell of the valleys where history and romance combine with rare natural beauty to make superb vacation territory.

Unfortunately the trip up the Hudson cannot be begun where the channel cut by the river really starts, for geologists tell us that this beginning is not at Manhattan Island, but one hundred miles out at sea. A prosaic pamphlet issued by the State of New York is brightened by a passage written by Dr. John M. Clarke, which tells of this inaccessible portion of the Hudson's course. Why should his sentences be permitted to doze in an official pamphlet? Here they are:

"When finding its way south before New York was born, the river turned prophetically a little toward the east, as if to greet the coming Verazzano and Hudson ...Thus it left the coming metropolis as far inland as Kingston is today and fell at length over the Continental ledge into the lap of the sea, one hundred miles beyond its present mouth...Into the solid granite heart of the high southern plateau it cut a gorge so long and deep that only half its work is visible to us. Here in front of us the old rock bottom lies buried nearly a thousand feet beneath the water, and out beyond New York runs that buried canyon which, if above the sea line today, would be comparable among the phenomena of our continent only to the Canyon of the Colorado."

Most of those who approach the Hudson River are as ignorant of the existence of such a canyon beneath

139

SEEING THE EASTERN STATES

the waves as they are of the Ambrose Channel cut
during long years through the shoals of the Lower Bay,
a channel so large that—it has been estimated— if a
similar cut were made through the heart of New York
City there would be a swath nearly as wide as Central
Park, stretching from one end of Manhattan Island
nearly to the other end, and fifteen feet deep!

For the purpose of the navigator and the tourist
the mouth of the Hudson lies far beyond the buried
canyon and the Ambrose Channel, beyond Staten Island,
whose possession was long a question between New
York and New Jersey, past Bedloe's Island, with its
welcoming Statue of Liberty, and on to what is
called North River because the Dutch so distinguished it from the South River, (or Delaware), which
flowed south of the Dutch settlements in New Jersey,
as the Hudson River flowed to the north of them.

The palatial river steamer makes its stately way between the amazing sky line of New York City and the
great docks on the Jersey shore. Then the green of
Riverside Drive and the varied architecture of Morning-
side Heights call the passenger to the Manhattan shore.
But the eye is lured from the shores by the sight of the
busy tugs that dart here and there, the sturdy ferry-
boats, the trim yachts anchored in the stream awaiting
the leisure of their owners, the warships with their
crews in white, the fleets or barges from the Erie Canal.

A few miles to its north the arm of the bay called
Harlem River, which connects with East River, passes
off from the Hudson to its task of completing the
water-circuit of Manhattan Island.

This is the origin of the Palisades. For more than
an hour they rise in majesty, claiming and holding the

attention of passengers who rejoice in the prospect from below, just as those who move along the heights think with gratitude that the Architect of the World had an eye for beauty when he did his work.

The Palisades are still at their best when the Hudson begins the broad swelling which the Dutch called the Tappan Zee. It is four miles across the broad bosom of the waters to Sunnyside, where Washington Irving lived, two miles below Tarrytown, with Sleepy Hollow close by, and the old Dutch church that dates from 1690.

Close to Tarrytown is Ossining, the beauty spot where those outside of the prison walls can look west into the country close to beautiful Rockland Lake, or north to Croton, a name familiar because of the reservoir back in the mountains from which New York long drew its sole supply of cool, clear water.

It is not enough to pass along this stretch of river by boat. The railroad on the bank must then be taken. Which bank? Both banks! Jutting rocks and jagged shores threaten to interrupt progress, but there are tunnels galore, and there are cuts and fills that make possible the continued onward rush when it looks as if it would be necessary to take the back track. From the train on the east bank the longing passenger thinks he must see more closely what the railroad on the west bank has to offer. And when he goes to the west bank he will feel just as eager about the east bank. So take the boat and also take the trains, first on one bank, then on the other.

Some of the names in this region where the Dutch flourished so long ago are as diverting as the scenery. There is Peekskill, for instance. Once John Peak

141

made his home on the creek, but he called the creek a
kill, so the name was easily fashioned. Isn't it fortunate they didn't have creeks in the Hudson country
in his day?

Other names are just as exciting, but they are not
always so easily accounted for. But why try to account
for Dunderberg and its neighbor, Anthony's Nose?
It is enough to enjoy the rugged uplift called Stony
Point, where Mad Anthony Wayne won fame in 1779,
or the crowning glory of the river, Storm King, the
monarch that stoops to bathe his feet in the waters
and lifts his head to the blue sky that seems to come
down to meet him.

But before Storm King's huge bulk is reached, miles
of the west bank must be examined. Old Fort Montgomery, close to Bear Mountain, is on the north bank
of Popolopen Creek. The railroad crosses it at a lower
level, but the highway uses a slender bridge high up
above the gorge—five feet higher than Brooklyn Bridge.
Far below in the quiet waters of the creek rides at
anchor the replica of Hudson's *Half Moon,* the central
feature of the Fulton Celebration in 1909. On the
other side of the bridge an old grist mill seems proper
company for the vessel of other days. And just
beyond, by the railroad's side, another relic shows
against the green of the trees—the wire carrier that
brings down to the dock by the waterside the iron from
the Forest of Dean Iron Mine, five miles back in the
hills. Since the days of the Revolution the iron has
sought the river for transportation to those who
valued highly the ninety-eight-per-cent-pure ore from
the hills.

Highland Falls are close enough to West Point to

make this a favorite excursion point for the cadets at the United States Military Academy. The fortunate young men have many such resorts. In other days one of these was Constitution Island, out in the river, where lived Susan Warner, author of the "Wide, Wide World," and her sister Anne.

Constitution Island was the terminus of the great chain stretched across the river in April, 1778, designed to make impossible the progress of the British vessels up the stream. The chain weighed one hundred and eighty-six tons; some of the links weighed one hundred and eighty pounds each. Fortunately a section of this chain has been preserved; it is one of the out-of-door exhibits at the West Point Military Academy.

It seems as if the Hudson opposite Constitution Island was made for defense. From the eastern bank there is a projection that reaches within fourteen hundred feet of the tongue of land thrust out from the mountain on the west. On this tongue fortifications were erected in Revolutionary days, where academic buildings have succeeded them.

The importance of this strategic point was recognized both by the British and the Continentals. Fortunately Washington and his men succeeded, in spite both of manly effort and treachery, in holding the region whose permanent capture might have meant the loss of the Revolution.

The pointed plateau whose near neighbors are Cro' Nest, Storm King, and Breakneck Mountain, was part of the grant made in 1723 by the English Crown to Charles Congreve. There are fourteen hundred and sixty-two acres in the tract. The land was still owned privately during the Revolution, but in 1780 Congress purchased it as the site for a permanent military fort, for eleven thousand and eighty-five dollars. Twenty-two years later the Military Academy was founded.

Anthony Trollope called West Point "the prettiest spot on the Hudson—the prettiest spot on the continent." Then he asked what right the authorities had to take "one of the prettiest spots which Nature, with all her vagaries, ever formed, and shut it up from all the world for purposes of war."

When the fortunes of West Point were in the balance, Washington, from his headquarters at Newburgh, kept in constant communication with the fortifications. Only four miles separated the Commander in Chief from the Gibraltar of the Hudson, but the road was far from easy. Storm King rose huge between. Thirty miles around the mountain his messenger had to go. And for nearly a century and a half this detour was necessary—until the State Highway Commission succeeded in building a magnificent road around the mountain that affords some of the most inspiring views in all the Hudson River region, far down to the river, off among the mountains, across the valleys. Don't miss the ride around the shoulders of Storm King!

But it is a mistake to think that beauty of river and mountains are left behind with Storm King. Newburgh claims attention not only because of its scenery, but because there the Headquarters, long occupied by Washington, are preserved by the State for the attention of the patriotic. And from Newburgh, past Poughkeepsie—where is to be seen the Clinton Mansion, occupied by George Clinton, first governor of the State—to Kingston—site of the Senate House, built in 1676, meeting place of the first State Senate

144

LOOKING UP AUSABLE CHASM, NEW YORK

AIR VIEW OF WEST POINT, NEW YORK
From the South

ALBANY, NEW YORK
Looking up State Street

in 1797—the speeding panorama of mountain and valley on either side of the narrowing stream helps mightily, in the thought of many, to make the Hudson supreme among American rivers.

Kingston is the southern gateway to the Catskills, whose summits rise one above another off to the west. It is difficult to resist their eloquent plea to leave the river and investigate their mysterious peaks and valleys, but the river's call is urgent, as it was to Henry Hudson, who took the *Half Moon* almost as far as the site of Hudson, the town that looks out on the reed-grown shallows that separate the channel from the west bank.

Above Hudson to Albany the river is quieter and the surroundings are more sedate. But even here let no one imagine that the real attractions of the Hudson have ceased. Albany, from its hill crowned by the Capitol, looks out on the stream at a point where the tide usually runs two feet. And this one hundred and fifty miles from the sea!

Beyond Albany the surroundings of the river are rugged in the extreme. The entrance of the Erie Canal at Troy is quiet, but the entrance of the Mohawk at Cohoes is after the water has been disturbed by a plunge over a ledge of rocks that reach from bank to bank. From the east comes the Hoosick River, another attractive stream whose cataracts have been utilized for driving the wheels of some of the mills that seek the banks of these rivers in such profusion. And off to the northwest of the point where the Hoosick enters the Hudson is famous Saratoga Springs, once the most noted watering place in America, now, after years of comparative neglect, on the way to more triumphant rule than ever.

New York State has become proprietor of hundreds of acres of the land on which the springs and wells are located, and the development of the new Saratoga has begun. As in the days before the Civil War, thousands of health-seekers as well as pleasure finders are going to the region where they have only to go to the top of Mount McGregor to see one of the finest panoramas New York State has to offer—the Hudson Valley to the east; the Adirondack foothills to the west; the Catskills, far to the south; the Green Mountains to the east.

Down on the banks of the Hudson is Schuylerville, where Burgoyne surrendered on that day of 1777 when hope dawned for America. "Within the territory of New York there is no more memorable spot," George William Curtis has said.

Another of the famous spots of the upper Hudson is Fort Edward, between Schuylerville and Glens Falls, where a fort was built in 1755. There, during the expedition against Canada, troops left the river for the twelve-mile portage to Wood Creek. But the popular fame of Fort Edward rests less in its military history than on the tragedy of Jane McCrea, an American girl, a dweller on the banks of the Hudson, who, in an attempt to pass through the English lines to meet the man to whom she was engaged, was captured by two bands of Indians. In a quarrel over who should have the honor of taking her to her lover she was slain. She lies buried in a little cemetery between Hudson Falls and Fort Edward. Indignation at her fate led to such an increase in the American forces that Burgoyne's defeat became possible soon afterward.

Just above Fort Edward, at Glens Falls, the Hudson, turning at right angles on itself, begins its long southerly course, after making a winding track from its source in the Adirondacks. But the turn is not made without tumult. For some distance the stream dashes over curiously shaped rocks, foams in and out of caverns, and in various ways seems to express its disapproval of the necessity of changing its direction. James Fenimore Cooper gave fame to these vagaries of the stream when, in writing "The Last of the Mohicans," he described the rocks and the tumbling waters. Access to the caverns of which he wrote is made easy by a circular staircase which leads from the handsome concrete bridge across the stream.

Glens Falls—called Wing's Falls until they became the property of John Glen in 1788—is in historic territory, for it is at the beginning of the old land route from the Hudson to Lake George, used by so many of the pioneer soldiers in their passage from Fort Edward to Fort William Henry, whose ruins are on the Lake George Battlefield Reservation, close to Lake George village, at the foot of the lake which has been called Lake Sacrament, Canideriout and Horicon. Francis Parkman, who was fascinated by the loveliness of its surroundings, called it "the Como of the Wilderness."

Fort William Henry was destroyed by Montcalm within two years of its building by General Johnson, who overcame the French through listening to the advice of an Indian chief; the chief urged him not to divide his forces against the enemy. Overlooking the lake

147

there is a monument crowned by the figures of the military leader and the Indian.

From the height where the monument stands there is a first rare glimpse of the lake set deep in a maze of crowding green mountains. For more than thirty miles the waters stretch away to the north, sometimes several miles wide, again narrow as a medium-sized river. Everywhere green islands dot the surface of the water, here singly, there in clusters, but always beguiling. Among these islands the steamer picks its way daintily, often exercising great care lest the wash injure the gems of green. But the danger of injury to the islands has been lessened by the building on many of them of dikes of stone. This work has been done under the direction of the New York State Conservation Commission, which owns more than one hundred and fifty of them. Campers are welcomed to these islands.

The western shore of the lake slopes rapidly up to the mountains which lead back at once into the Adirondack wilderness. "Do not go back into the forests without a guide," warning is giving persistently to visitors. But there are sure to be some unwise pilgrims who know better than those acquainted with the region; they persist in wandering alone where they are so sure they can find their way. Some of them have been lost for hours and even days; others have not come back at all.

There is danger on the lake as well as back from the lake, but this danger also may be avoided easily by those who listen to warning words. The surface of the water looks so calm and smooth, under ordinary circumstances, that the temptation is to go far from

148

land in a canoe or a sailboat. But sorrow has come to many who have yielded to this temptation. For sudden storm swoops down from the mountains, the waves are stirred up quickly to great heights, and nothing but the staunchest vessel can live in the tumult The author remembers going from a near-by island to Sabbath Day Point. On the way it was remarked how smooth the water was, how blue the sky. Fifteen minutes after landing the sky grew black, the wind rose, darkness shut out a sailboat half a mile off shore —and when the light came again the sailboat was bottom side up. In half an hour the sky was serene once more and the waters were returning to their accustomed placidity.

The three hours required for the steamer ride along Lake George are made memorable by passing the Tongue, the mountain promontory that extends far into the water; Shelving Rock; Black Mountain, two thousand feet high; and Sabbath Day Point, a pleasing projection where, in 1776, General Abercrombie, on his way to attack the French at Ticonderoga with one thousand boats and sixteen thousand men, paused to spend Sunday.

Toward the head of the lake the steamboat passes between two great rocky precipices, walls for its narrowing channel. The rock on the right is Anthony's Slide; that on the left is Rogers' Rock. The story is told that, one day in 1758, Major Rogers, pursued by Indians, reached the summit of the rock, far above the water. In the few moments when he was out of their sight he sent his pack sliding down the hundred feet of perfectly smooth rock to the bit of beach by the waterside. Then he reversed his snowshoes and retraced

149

his steps. The Indian thought he had gone to his death, but a little later he was able to recover his pack from the beach and to hurry away to safety.

During the four-mile interval between Lake George and Lake Champlain the water falls two hundred and thirty feet. The route is now rugged, now quiet, but always beautiful.

Lake George really overlaps Lake Champlain for a distance of twenty miles, but the lower reaches of the latter lake are so narrow, and the upper reaches are so rarely beautiful, that the miles below Fort Ticonderoga may be disregarded by the pilgrim who would follow in the path of the Indian and the pioneer.

Samuel de Champlain was the first white man to come to the site of Fort Ticonderoga, which is not far from the village of the same name. The Iroquois Indians, with whom he engaged on July 1, 1609, close to the site of the fort, called the spot Cheonderoga, or Sounding Waters; probably this name was due to the noise of the Lower Falls, by which the waters from Lake George make the final plunge to the level of Lake Champlain.

Not until 1755 did the French decide to fortify the plateau on the point that rises about one hundred feet above the lake and looks across the water to the low-lying shore beyond. The name they gave this stronghold, Fort Carillon, was changed to Ticonderoga in 1759, when the British troops occupied it. The flag of Great Britain was flung to the breeze above the walls until 1775, when Ethan Allen and his Green Mountain Boys captured the fort by a daring exploit concerning which truth and fiction have been busy ever since.

During the next few years the two flags alternated in an interesting manner.

The days of picturesque ruin ended in 1909 when the patriotic owner of the land began the restoration of a portion of the fort in season for the Tercentenary Celebration of the visit of Champlain.

From Ticonderoga northward every mile of the shore is historic. Crown Point is near, and so is the site of Fort St. Frederic, built by the French in 1731. Above these landmarks the lake increases both in width and in wild beauty. The mountains come closer, crowding the water into narrow passages, scenes of many conflicts between the savages with their French Allies and the English and Americans. Split Rock Mountain, surmounted by Split Rock Light, is one of the finest spots on the lake to look off to the west to the Adirondacks, or far away to the east where the Green Mountains lift their peaks. Then the lake becomes generously broad as if to make as delightful as possible the vision from the heights of Burlington. There are partisans who say there is not on the continent a finer view than that from the campus of the University of Vermont.

And Burlington people find it an easy matter to follow where that view leads them. An accommodating steamboat crosses the lake to Port Kent. Then an electric line provides passage to Ausable Chasm, a marvel in the rocks to which Baedeker in his guidebook has given two stars, an honor reserved by him for less than a dozen spots in the entire country.

Ausable Chasm is an unexpected development in a comparatively placid stream. There is nothing especially remarkable about the Ausable until it drops

151

headlong over a seventy foot precipice and swirls into Buttermilk Falls, seventy feet high. Then the waters find themselves far down between great precipices, and they champ and chafe and fret in their confinement like wild beasts in captivity. In its winding gorge falls and cascades, rocks and whirlpools come too fast for count. Picturesque names have been given to many of the outstanding points of interest, but they are not as picturesque as the spots themselves: for instance, Mystic Gorge, the Devil's Oven, Pulpit Rock, Jacob's Ladder, the Smuggler's Pass, Table Rock. The names can be duplicated, but not the spots in the chasm of which they tell. Perhaps they will satisfy until the opportunity has come to walk above them, to pass among them, or to sit in a boat while a skilful waterman shoots the rapids with perfect nonchalance, while breathless passengers hold fast to the boat, only in a moment to wish that they could have the thrill all over again.

But when the deceptive waters of the Ausable enter Champlain a short distance beyond the point where they make such a tumult, they are as peaceful as the bosom of the lake when there is not a breath of wind.

Ten miles south of the mouth of the Ausable, on Cumberland Bay, a German nobleman, Count Vredenburg, located before the Revolution on thirty thousand acres of land. His house and sawmill were at Vredenburg Falls, on the Saranac, several miles from the present city of Plattsburg. The Count disappeared in time for Judge Platt to patent the land and make a settlement that was to preserve his name, on one of the choicest sites on the lake. Thirty years later, on September 11, 1814, Captain Thomas Macdonough made the bay famous when his squadron defeated a

152

THE NARROWS, LAKE GEORGE, NEW YORK

British squadron under Captain George Downie, and so helped to check the progress of the thirteen thousand men who had come thus far from Canada in the attempt to invade New York State.

The upper portion of the lake on which so many attempts were made by invaders can be seen best by railroad—a remarkable railroad, extending from Burlington to Alburgh directly across the islands that divide Champlain into two parts. There are thirty-seven miles of journey—all within Vermont—that for scenic splendor send to the rear the Lucin Cut-Off on Great Salt Lake and even the Key West Extension of the Florida East Coast Railroad.

The schedule has been arranged so that, in June, the train leaves Burlington at an hour when the mysteries of the night are slowly yielding to the glories of the day. The rising sun is reflected in the waters as the railroad leaps from the mainland to the south end of Grand Isle (or South Hero Island) over a fill more than four miles long, constructed on a curve so as to get the benefit of the sand bar. Of course the engineer did not think how the route chosen would add to the beauty of the ride! But those who sit at the window on the right side of the train can appreciate both the triumph of the builders and the unusual scenery. As the train passes swiftly across its island, the thoughts turn to the first settler, Ebenezer Allen, who, in 1777, at Shelburne Point, led a company of men who took from British troops a number of prisoners. Among these was a negro woman and child. Knowing that slavery was forbidden by the Constitution, he wrote "to whom it may concern:"

"According to a Resolve Past by the Honorable

Continental Congress that all Prisses belong to the
Captivators thereof, therefore she and her Child became
the just Property of the Captivators thereof."

So he set them both free—"I being Conscihentious
that it is not Right in the Sight of God to Keep Slaves,"
he wrote.

For seven miles the railroad follows Grand Isle, the
old home of the manumitter, sometimes close to the
lake, where there are glimpses of the water, other
islands and the eastern shore; sometimes farther inland, among the lands of those who, until the building
of the railroad during the early years of the twentieth
century, had no communication with the mainland
except by boat.

The gap to North Hero Island leads across the
channel to Pilot's Knob, a narrow, wooded ridge that
precedes the fine rolling lands where farmers share with
cottagers the pleasures of the summer in the fairyland
amid the waters.

One of the first official records referring to this
island, as well as its neighbor to the south, was made
to the "General Assembly of the State of Vermont" in
1779, in a petition that "Humbly Shueth that Wharas
there is a Large tract of Land the jint Property of the
State in Pertickler...two large Ilands lying in the
Lake Champlain betwine Crown Pint and Canaday
South line...about Anaf for two town Ships." Having made this introduction the petition concluded, "We
yeour Hanners Petisners Prey in behalf of our Selves
and others that the two a bove s'd Ilans be granted
to us and a Sutible Number of settlers with all the
Good Regalation town ships as your Honners shal see
fite in your Grate Wisdom..."

154

A third deep fill has on the west green Isle La Motte, called the "Little Gem of the Lake," named for Captain La Motte, who built there the French fort St. Anne in 1665, and on the east the wasp-like "Carrying Place" of North Hero, where of old smugglers eluded authorities pursuing in more unwieldy craft by the simple expedient of crossing the narrow neck of land and reembarking on the other side, in effect miles from their hunters, though actually but a tantalizingly short distance away. This fill enables the railroad to take the mainland where the Tongue reaches down from the Alburgh peninsula.

After a few miles more on the peninsula the railroad turns west, crossing the Richelieu River into New York State by a trestle a mile long, from which there is, to the south, a last glimpse of the hundred-mile-long lake, while to the north loom up the stone walls of Fort Montgomery, called Fort Blunder because, in 1818, only a few years after it was built, careful surveys showed that it was just over the line in Canada. The land on which the fort stands was ceded by treaty to the United States in 1842.

Thus from United States territory the fort frowns harmlessly down on the last miles of the grand passage from the St. Lawrence to the lakes that lead to the Hudson—the historic route, through three centuries, of countless thousands, intent on errands both of peace and war.

CHAPTER XVII

IN ADIRONDACK WILDS

IT is the boast of New Yorkers that, while the Adirondack Mountains may not be as grand or as lofty as the Rocky Mountains, they are at any rate the country's oldest mountains. They call attention to the assurances of the geologists that the peaks of these mountains peeped out of the sea as rock islands long before convulsions of nature produced the Rockies, which must therefore be content to be "also rans" in the race for priority.

But it is not necessary for the possessors of the mountains of northeastern New York to be too modest in their claims as to the beauty and nobility of proud eminences like Mount Marcy, one hundred and four feet more than a mile in height, which cherishes Lake Tear in the Clouds, the ultimate source of the Hudson River. The Indians called the mountain Tahawus, the Cloud Piercer, but in late days it has been condemned to bear the more prosaic name of the early Governor of New York, William L. Marcy, one of whose claims to fame is that he first used the phrase, "To the victor belongs the spoils," though a better claim is that he helped pass the law that gave a free library to every one of New York's school districts.

Facing Marcy is Haystack, with the gloomy Panther Gorge between, and a short distance to the west lofty Mt. McIntyre and rocky Mt. Colden have separated themselves just far enough to make that favorite path-

AVALANCHE LAKE IN WINTER
Between Mt. Colden and Mt. McIntyre, New York

FROM THE SUMMIT OF MT. SEWARD, NEW YORK
Long Lake in Distance

way of Indians who sought the North, Avalanche Pass. The walls rise abruptly on either side, and Avalanche Lake—loftiest lake in New York State—fills the gap. From the precipices on either side avalanches thunder down into the waters, making the passage dangerous during the season of ice and snow.

Another pass that was famous in the days of the Iroquois is Indian Pass, a gorge shadowed by Mounts McNaughton, Henderson and Santanoni. Mt. Henderson has as neighbor on the north rock-walled Wallface, as well as Mt. Seward, whose forest-covered twin peaks show to perfection the fifteen-mile stretch of Long Lake —a widening of Raquette River—with mountain ridges on either side and wooded islands like emeralds on its winding silver ribbon.

Down to the south of Long Lake, Blue Mountain peeps down on Blue Mountain Lake, where islands large and islands small scattered carelessly about look like bits of the mountain slopes located where they can be most effective as parts of a picture that would have enraptured the poets of England's famous Lake District.

To name even one-tenth of the lakes and mountain peaks of the Adirondacks would be a tedious task; there are nearly two thousand mountains and fifteen hundred lakes in the Couch-sa-ra-ge or Dismal Wilderness of the Iroquois, which is bounded, roughly, by the Mohawk and the Black Rivers, Lake Ontario and the St. Lawrence, Lake Champlain, Lake George, and the Hudson River. Access to this region of endless delight is made easy not only by these waterways, but by railroads, as well as by highways that penetrate to every part. Details of these roads are given in the Recreation Circular, "Adirondack Highways," published by the New

York Conservation Commission at Albany. Special attention is given to that portion—the lion's share—of the mountain paradise set apart by the State as Adirondack Park.

A second fascinating booklet issued by the Commission tells of the wonderful Adirondack Canoe Routes that start at Old Forge, little more than fifty miles from Utica, and—with a few brief portages that really add zest to the sport—lead through the Fulton Chain, to Raquette Lake and Forked Lake, Raquette River and Long Lake, Raquettte River once more, and Tupper Lake, or to the Saranacs.

Equipped with the canoeing booklet, supplemented by the eighteen five-cent sheets of the United States Geological Survey which tell in detail of the lakes by the way, the vacation seeker should not fail to find the satisfaction due him who longs for days on the water where fish are plentiful, where beaver abound and deer come down to drink, where the birches may yet be found in all their silver glory.

Those who appreciate the birch tree have a warm feeling for the Indian guide of whom an Adirondack tramper told. One day the tramper reached up to get a birch bark cup from a tree near the camp, directly on the trail. But the Indian said, "Wait, me go back." In a few minutes he returned with a cup he had fashioned from bark gathered on a tree that was invisible from the trail. Ashamed, the tramper said, "You did not want me to take bark from a tree near the trail?" "No, too pretty!" was the reply of the savage whose people had never dreamed of desecrating the wilderness.

With the coming of the white man some of the glories of the wild began to disappear. Once deer were plentiful there, but as early as 1709 it became necessary to make a close season for deer in Suffolk County, and in 1788 the close season was extended to the entire state. As the years passed, the law was more rigidly enforced, but by 1919 it was estimated that there were only about fifty thousand deer in the state. That year more than sixty thousand hunters entered the mountains—more than one for each deer! They had pleaded for a relaxing of the law so that does as well as bucks might be killed. One of the arguments was that no one would kill a doe when he could secure a buck. Yet official investigation of the trophies of many hunters who left the mountain country showed three does killed to one buck. If continued, such slaughter soon would have exterminated the white-tailed deer.

A few years ago it was feared that the beaver had been exterminated by wholesale trapping. In 1895 there were very few beaver in the state. A law protecting the survivors was passed, and in 1921 there were nearly twenty thousand of the busy beaver on the watercourses, and probably at least one thousand dams. The damage done by the little creatures became so great that the destruction of some of them, within strictly prescribed limits, was urged. Many of their dams that led to the killing of trees, and the overflow of highways, were destroyed. But more energetic measures became necessary, because the beaver would restore a dam in a single night.

Legends linger about the lakes where the beaver are so busy. But better even than legends are tales like that which has given Saranac Lake renown for heroism as well as for beauty. This is the story of

SEEING THE EASTERN STATES

Edward Livingstone Trudeau, the New York City physician who, in 1873, was told that he had not long to live. He sought the Adirondacks, not because he thought the climate would help him, but because of his delight in the forest primeval. On the forty-two-mile ride down from Ausable Forks to Paul Smith's he had to lie on a mattress. At Paul Smith's he was greeted by strong, healthy men who little thought that forty years later most of them would be dead, while he would still be in the mountains.

The open-air life restored him miraculously. Soon he was caring for a few patients—an injured guide, perhaps, or some of the summer guests who needed him. When he removed to Saranac Lake, several invalids from the city came to seek his aid. As he treated them and their successors, there developed gradually the dream of a sanitarium where patients who sought the mountains, hoping to arrest consumption, might find winter accommodations. His dream found its first realization in 1884, when he opened the Adirondack Cottage Sanitarium.

The site chosen was on the side of Pisgah Mountain, where the unbroken forest, rising abruptly from the river, and the extensive sweep of the valley, made a deep impression on him. The guests, who had learned to love him, clubbed together and bought sixteen acres on the favored spot.

For more than a quarter of a century Dr. Trudeau served others, and before he died he had the joy of seeing the hospital grow until it was giving hope and life to scores and hundreds.

Dr. Trudeau's hospital at Saranac Lake, the largest village in the Adirondacks, is close to Lower Saranac
160

Lake, which is thought to be a marvel of surpassing beauty until Lake Placid is seen. Then Saranac is not displaced in the affections; it is only coupled with another glory of the mountains. And as acquaintance is extended, the list of favorites also is extended. For it is impossible to select one of the Adirondack lakes and say of it, "This is the finest."

Numbers of mountains and lakes are passed in the course of a railroad journey from the head of Lake Champlain at Rouse's Point to Utica—the only railroad route that cuts across the entire Adirondack region. First it traverses a high plateau around the edge of the mountains. Forests are everywhere, and rocks— sometimes scattered aimlessly, again a rock floor for the plateau or outcroppings that look like the foundations of some giant's castle. Here and there the plateau is broken by some stream that has cut a way far below the surface. Soon after leaving Malone the railroad is in the midst of the mountains. Rounded summits rise on either hand, but particular attention is attracted by Owl's Head, on the right of the track, named because there is a fancied resemblance to the bird of the night. Other mountains like many-humped camels appear, with lakes so enticing that it is difficult to remain on the train.

If, when Utica is reached, the conscience is troubled because the journey through the Adirondacks has been made too quickly, a good way to satisfy it is by going on to Oswego, there taking the steamer to the lower end of Lake Ontario, and along the stretch of the St. Lawrence included in the St. Lawrence Reservation set apart by New York. The reservation, which includes the Thousand Islands, is matched by the reservation on the Canadian side of the river. Thus both banks and all the islands are included in an International Park, dedicated to the pleasure of the people. The Indians, with their usual genius for giving names, called this favored region Monatoana, "The Garden of the Great Spirit." To the English it became "the Lake of a Thousand Islands," for the river, just as it leaves the lake, is fifteen miles wide, while a dozen miles or more farther on it is still four miles wide.

Most of the islands are in private hands, but their owners coöperate with the state authorities, who control various parks on the shore as well as islands on the stream, so that there is a generous welcome to those who come to see the seventeen hundred islands. If their approach is by the Roosevelt Memorial Highway that skirts the shore of the river—a section of the longer highway from Portland, Maine, to Portland, Oregon—they will pass close to some of the state parks, one of them directly opposite Carleton Island, where may still be seen the ruins of Fort Haldimand, built by the British during the Revolution.

When the project for the St. Lawrence outlet from the Great Lakes to the Sea is carried out by the building of dams and canals, these islands of the International Park will be passed by thousands of ocean vessels that will carry the products of the western farms from the prairies to European markets, and thus there will be forged another link in the chain that binds together the people to the north of the St. Lawrence and the nation to the south.

CHAPTER XVIII

THROUGH THE LONG HOUSE OF THE IROQUOIS

From Troy to Buffalo

WHEN the Iroquois Indians of what is now New York State were in their glory, their old men used to tell around their council fires of the time when their ancestors, long confined under a mountain near the falls of the Oswego River, were released by the Holder of the Heavens, Ta-reng-a-wa-gon. By him they were directed to the country between the Hudson River and Lake Erie. The Mohawks lived to the eastward, then came the Oneidas, the Onondagas, the Cayugas and the Senecas. All went well with them until enemies from the north attacked the Onandagas. They appealed to Ta-reng-a-wa-gon, and he urged them to call a council of the Five Nations, who should then band together as brothers. A council was held on the shores of Onondaga Lake, and the Five Nations organized Ko-no-shi-o-ni, the Long House. The Mohawks agreed to guard the eastern door, while to the Senecas was given charge of the western door. The capital, the seat of the Council Fire, was in the territory of the Onondagas, a few miles south of the present site of Syracuse.

But while the story of the origin of the Long House is legendary, the Long House itself was a vivid reality. In their fair chosen territory, "the Romans of the New World," as they have been called, hunted in time of peace and hurried hither and thither in time of war. From north to south and from east to west, so Fiske says, "the bronzed warriors of the famous federation traveled swiftly and struck silently." And they maintained their hold on this territory until 1768, when the treaty of Fort Stanwix opened the country from Lake Ontario to the Delaware. But even yet their names are graven from east to west of what was the Long House—on the Mohawk River, and on four of the lakes that are embosomed in the heart of New York State.

The Mohawk's entrance to the Hudson is close to Troy, the manufacturing city at the head of tidewater on the Hudson River that stretches along the stream for seven miles. From these highlands the warriors of the Iroquois often looked on the sweeping Mohawk. Those who have come after them see not only the river, but also the Erie Canal, completed in 1825 from Lake Erie to the Hudson River.

The eastern door to the country through which the canal was cut was a movable affair, for Schenectady, west of Troy, was once called Schoo, a contraction probably of Schonowe, Indian for the gate. It is most certainly the entrance to a region of beauty, fertility and picturesqueness by many thought beyond comparison. The valley of the Mohawk, stretching away toward Lake Ontario, is an artist's paradise.

In this glorious Mohawk country the Indians took delight. But sometimes the braves hearkened to the call of the Delaware and the Chesapeake, where they had hunting grounds. Then a favored route of travel was from the Mohawk near the site of Canajoharie to Otsego Lake, and so to the Susquehanna. On the way they passed a depression in the trail where now is

Cherry Valley. There, in 1738, Samuel Dunlop, a minister from Ireland, attracted by the peaceful valley, on the edge of the rugged country, settled his little colony from New Hampshire on eight thousand acres, received from the Indians. And there they remained in peace until that awful day in 1778 when Brant and his Indians fell on the frontier settlement, killed some of the people, and drove the rest to Schenectady. A tablet on the Presbyterian Church at Cherry Valley tells the story.

One of the sources of the Susquehanna has its beginning close to Cherry Valley. Another comes from Otsego Lake, famous because in the valley to the south, at Cooperstown, James Fenimore Cooper was born. There he spent his boyhood, and in the vicinity he wrote many of his novels. But for many years he was the most unpopular man on the lake. This was due to his innocent attempts to preserve his rights to a beauty-spot on the shore, called Three-mile Point, because of the distance from Cooperstown. In legal form he asserted his rights to the Point, but promised to grant the use of the property to all who would ask his permission. The villages opposed "the arrogant pretensions of one James Fennimore Cooper" for they proposed to continue to use the Point "without being indebted to the liberality of anyone, whether native or foreigner."

The result was a demand for the removal of Cooper's novels from the Cooperstown Library, and a series of attacks that were made the basis of libel suits from 1838 to 1844.

Sometimes Cooper's heroes went to the Mohawk country, which is at its best to the north of Otsego Lake and westward to Utica. There, in Forest Hill

Cemetery, is a memorial of the heroic days of which the novelist told—the Sacred Stone of the Oneida Indians, which for generations was the gathering place for those who would take counsel for the good of the Five Nations. In 1849, with the consent of the Oneidas, the stone was moved to the cemetery, where survivors of the tribe sometimes pay it a visit of ceremony.

North of Utica is a country that was famous many years ago, and that should be better known today. There West Canada Creek, coming down from its source in the lakes in the heart of the Adirondacks, descends 312 feet within two miles, between rock walls often as high as 150 feet. Several of the series of cataracts which are known as Trenton Falls are eighty feet high.

There was a day when no visit to America was thought complete without a pilgrimage to Trenton Falls. Visitors came to this from all sections of the country, as well as from abroad.

The Mohawk country to the south of Trenton Falls won a place in annals of the Revolution by an event that proved to be more momentous than participants in it thought at the time. At Herkimer, east of Utica, the seat of Fort Dayton, lived General Nicholas Herkimer. At Rome, forty miles to the west, Fort Stanwix sheltered troops which were a source of strength to the whole valley. In August, 1777, a force of about seventeen hundred whites and Indians, under General St. Leger, laid siege to the seven hundred Continentals in the fort, who were flying above it, the new flag adopted by the Continental Congress, which had been made from a white sheet, a soldier's blue coat, and strips from the red petticoat of a soldier's wife.

166

TRENTON FALLS, NEW YORK

GORGE OF THE GENESEE RIVER AT ROCHESTER, NEW YORK

IN THE HEART OF SYRACUSE, NEW YORK

Word of the peril of the men at the fort was carried to the old hero at Herkimer, who quietly assembled a force of militia and hastened up the valley toward Fort Stanwix. On August 6, when they were crossing a picturesque ravine two miles from the entrance into the Mohawk of Oriskany Creek, Herkimer's men were attacked by eight hundred troops under Joseph Brant. Then followed a brief conflict of which a British historian has said, "Oriskany, for the strength of the forces engaged, proved to be the bloodiest conflict of the entire war." Of the eight hundred surprised men, more than six hundred were either killed or wounded. Their leader, wounded at the beginning, directed the defense from the ground. Later he was taken back to his fortress home on the south bank of the Mohawk, near Herkimer, where he died.

The old homestead has been made a shrine by the state. His memory is further preserved by a monument at Herkimer; by fourteen stones that mark his route to Oriskany; and by a battle monument on a height by the side of the ravine, the scene of the conflict, called by some "the Thermopylæ of the American Revolution," for it led directly to the defeat of Burgoyne at Saratoga.

The monuments at Oriskany and Herkimer have companions not far away. At Clinton, not many miles from Utica, is a stone erected in commemoration of the treaty of Fort Stanwix, November 5, 1768, which opened to settlement a wide extent of the Indian country. At Steuben, in the center of a five-acre tract of woodland, stands the monument to Major General Frederick William Steuben, friend of the colonists in the Revolution, who died on a part of the sixteen thousand acre tract given him by New York because of his services, and at Rome is the memorial of the fort of the treaty, the fort besieged by St. Leger, which was built to guard the "carrying place" from the Mohawk to Wood Creek. This important stretch of three miles began at the western part of the sharp bend described by the Mohawk in its passage through the town.

Historically Rome is remarkable also, because, on the route of the old portage, the first spadeful of earth was turned by the builders of the Erie Canal. This was Rome's celebration of Independence Day, 1817. And on July 4, 1918, was celebrated the enlargement of the Canal for the accommodation of barges of one thousand tons burden.

The Indians called Rome Deo-wain-sta, "The Great Carrying Place." The English name was given to it because of the part taken there in the defense of the Republic. Thus it took its place with a notable company of New York cities, towns and villages, most of them in the central part of the state, which have classical names. Others are Ithaca, Syracuse, Utica, Troy, Aristotle, Attica, Aurelius, Carthage, Cato, Cicero, Euclid, Junius, Ovid, Palmyra, Penelope, Plato, Scipio, Solon, and Virgil!

Rome was not given its name for more than fifty years after St. Leger paid his disastrous visit to Fort Stanwix. The start for his expedition was made from Fort Oswego, on the shore of Lake Ontario, where the English had been in power for many years, with a brief interruption following 1756, when the French captured the stronghold.

The modern city dates from 1797, when the legislature set apart one hundred acres on the west side of the Oswego River, at its mouth, as the site of the town. Montcalm Park is a part of the original site.

An important section of the Barge Canal is between Oswego and Syracuse, the city situated in a delightful amphitheater of hills in the midst of which is Onondaga Lake. The settlement by the lakeside was famous in early days for its seemingly inexhaustible supplies of salt. Salt springs were spoken of by explorers in 1653. In 1797 the state leased the salt land, and found it a productive source of supply until long after the Civil War. As late as 1862 nine million barrels were produced. But in 1898 the lands were sold; other centers had displaced Syracuse in the production of the necessity. More diversified manufactures have made Syracuse independent of the dwindling supply.

Syracuse is on the edge of the famous Finger Lake District whose heart is where Seneca and Cayuga Lakes stretch southward in long, narrow valleys, fringed by wooded hills. To the south of the lakes are heights of from fifteen hundred to two thousand feet, the watershed between them and the Susquehanna valley.

The region between the heights of the central portion of the peaceful bodies of water is a wilderness of creeks and gorges and waterfalls; farther north the country becomes more quiet, but it is still of remarkable beauty. Those who have taken the railroad trip from Ithaca along the western shore of Cayuga Lake know something of the bewildering variety of the scenery, impressed on their minds by the fascinating glimpses of water far down through the trees that fringe the shore, including the reach across the lake where Cornell University students row with their rivals. Those who have taken automobile trips along the highways close to the lake can tell more of the amazing succession of natural wonders. But only those who have spent days in tramping through the valleys and along the streams can understand why geologists declare that this Finger Lake Country is one of the most remarkable in America.

The peculiar structure of the valleys—''hanging valleys'' they are called—tributary to the lakes is the explanation given of the variety of scenic features. This structure is similar in some respects to that of the Yosemite Valley. Through these valleys streams flow more or less sedately along until they reach an elevation of from eight hundred to nine hundred feet above the sea. Then they descend by picturesque falls and along dark and devious gorges to the level of the lake. Within a few miles of Ithaca are dozens of these hanging valleys, with their falls and gorges, and close to the south end of Seneca Lake are many more. Visitors to Cornell University and Ithaca know Falls Creek, at the boundary of the campus, spanned by a bridge high above the gorge, and close to the falls. Travelers on the Lehigh Valley Railroad have learned to look for lofty Taughannock Falls, from the bridge flung across the gorge. Watkins Glen, near the head of Seneca Lake, is familiar to many because the State Reservation, with its three miles of falls and cascades, bounded by rocky walls, is well advertised. But how many know of Excelsior Glen, Montour Falls, Hector Falls, Havana Glen, Cascadilla Creek, Newfield Creek, Trumansburg Creek, Salmon Creek, or the gorges that lead to little Cayuta Lake?

When the Finger Lake gorges are left behind by the traveler bound south to the Susquehanna, beauty is not ended, though the country is entirely different.

170

IN WATKINS GLEN, NEW YORK

CHAUTAUQUA LAKE, NEW YORK

First there is a wide valley, bounded by a succession of rounded hills, now high, now low. This is the country of starry fields of buckwheat. Then comes a narrower valley, bounded on either hand by rounded ridges where the evergreens mingle with the deciduous trees. Always a look backward or forward gives the impression of a closed-in valley; the twisting of the ridges makes them seem to obstruct passage in any direction.

But the journey westward from the north end of the lakes is altogether different. The country becomes less rugged, but it never for a moment loses its charm. One place is remarkable because of the gorge of the Genesee River, in the heart of Rochester, from fifty to two hundred feet high. The Falls of the Genesee are the center of interest, with their plunges of 96, 26 and 83 feet. And then during the seven miles from the city to the lake, the river drops 263 feet more! These falls and gorges are explained by geologists in the same manner as those at Niagara. The crossing of the river by the Erie Canal, on an arched viaduct, adds to the variety of the water picture in the city that was first called Falls Town, then Rochesterville.

But Rochester cannot claim all the worth-while part of the Genesee River. Perhaps fifty miles up the stream a State Reservation called Letchworth Park, containing one thousand acres, includes Portage Gorge and Portage Falls. Though little known in comparison, this reservation is well entitled to recognition with the Niagara Reservation by reason of its unusual charm.

Beyond the Genesee and Rochester the rolling country leads to Buffalo, the city which President McKinley called "the great doorway of the inland seas." Yet it is little more than a century since a

171

visitor to the shore of Lake Erie spoke slightingly of "Buffalo, a village of about sixteen houses near the outlet of Lake Erie," and added that it could be avoided by using a road that passed within two miles! Today who wants to avoid the city now famous for shady streets, pleasant homes, inviting boulevards and parks —from which the Keep off the Grass signs have all been removed,—as well as for tremendous business activity, both on land and on the water? The building near here—in 1679— of the *Griffon*, first vessel on the Great Lakes, and—in 1818—of the *Walk-in-the-Water*, first steamer on the Lakes, was a prophecy of its fame as a port, while the erection in 1843 of the first grain elevator in the world was a forecast of the industrial expansion on shore.

What a change since 1807, when the visitor to whom reference has already been made, said that there was then no symptom of industry! Surprised, he asked where was the market for the country that he thought should be tributary to Buffalo, and was informed that the traffic went through Buffalo to New Orleans by way of "Chataugu" Lake. The single portage of nine miles between Lake Erie and New Orleans—Chataugu Portage—made the route pleasing.

Once there was not even this land gap, for there was a time when the outlet of the lake that has given its name to popular lecture courses was into Lake Erie, and so to the Atlantic Ocean. The change came—so geologists say—when, during the Ice Age, debris deposited south of Chautauqua Lake forced it to seek an outlet by way of the Allegheny, the Ohio, the Mississippi, and the Gulf of Mexico.

CHAPTER XIX

WHERE NIAGARA'S WATER'S PLUNGE

ONE day in 1809 a lone horseback rider, who is known only as "T. C." passed through the Genesee Country in search of Niagara Falls. "You cannot miss them," was the assurance of a tavern-keeper in "Chippeway," on the Canadian side of the river; "they are by the roadside." And two miles farther on, when he came to Table Rock, he had his first view of the thundering cataract.

When he went back to the tavern he wrote a glowing description of what he had seen that might well have been penned by an observer more than a century later:

"The roaring and foaming of the rapids, for near a mile in full view before the river arrives at the precipice, the green tint of the water, edged all the way down by curly folds of snow-white foam, the chasm of boiling snow into which the river pours; the mist that eternally hovers over the gulf below, and through which you see at intervals the turbulence of the bottom; the rim of the island which divides the falls, and which seems to descend even below the edge of the precipice itself; the immense interminable mass of wood, which fills the whole of the surrounding country, and borders to the very edge of every part of the watery prospect; and the rapidity with which the green and white current below drives along as if in haste to escape from the terrible chasm in which it had been engulfed, form altogether a scene of grandeur and of beauty unrivalled.''

He was told of the pleasure to be gained from a view of the Falls by a descent to the rocks below, but when he learned that the only possible way was by a flimsy ladder, kept at a house near by, he decided not to attempt it.

Descent to the depths has been easy for late pilgrims, but Table Rock, from which "T. C." had his impressive view, crashed into the stream forty-one years after his visit, undermined by the swirling waters.

The fall of Table Rock was an indication of the way in which the great Niagara Gorge has been formed during a period that some geologists say was but five thousand years, while others insist it was from six to ten times as long, or more.

Lake Erie is nearly three hundred feet higher than Lake Ontario. Long ago the waters from the higher level reached the lower level at the escarpment, about six miles south of Ontario, plunging over a ledge of limestone that extends back toward Lake Erie and disappears under the lake. The water broke away the edge of the ledge and year by year the waterfall slowly receded. Then the Gorge formed gradually, until it reached back to the present location of the Falls. The rock is still wearing away, the recession of the Horseshoe Fall being estimated at four or five feet each year. The recession of the American Fall is not nearly so great.

The underlying rock, being softer, is hollowed out by the action of the waters at the foot of the Falls. The harder surface rock, undermined, drops into the

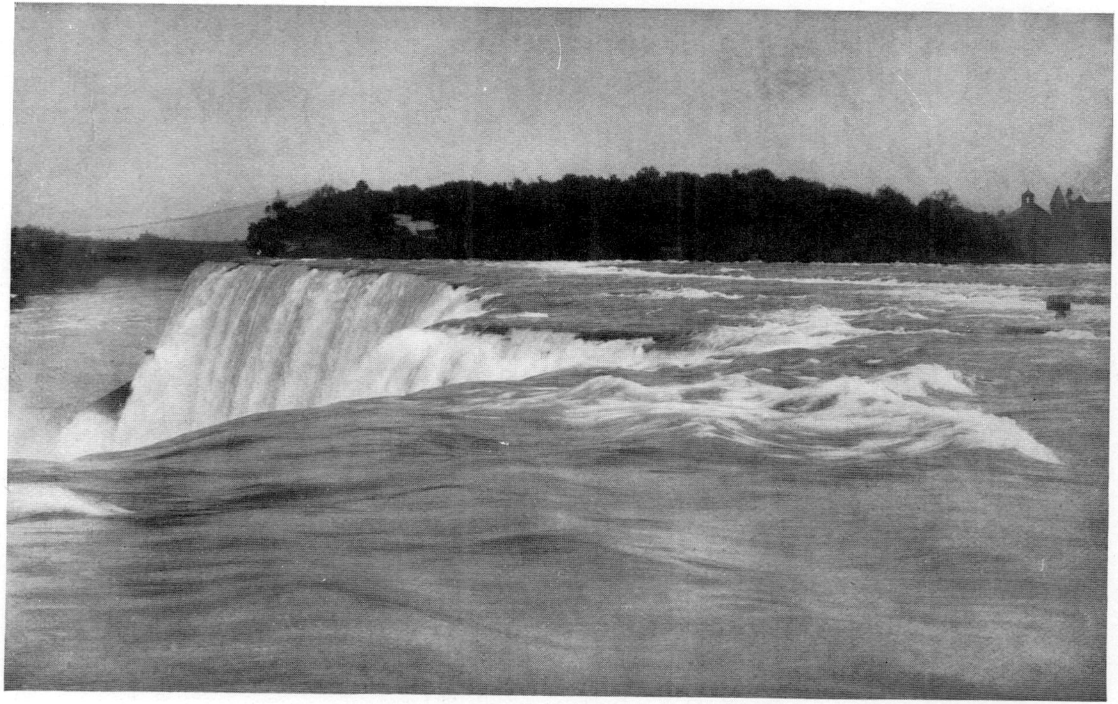

THE RAPIDS ABOVE HORSESHOE FALLS AT NIAGARA

THE AMERICAN FALLS AT NIAGARA

stream and is ground to powder by the water as it falls on them and churns above them.

The height of the American Fall is only 167 feet and of the Horseshoe Fall, 158 feet; the remainder of the descent to the level of Lake Ontario is accounted for by the fearful rapids above and below the Falls.

The modern visitor who would see the torrent in its majesty should follow in the steps of "T. C." and go to the Canadian side. Then he will have a wonderful sweep of a full mile, first the Horseshoe Fall, which is now more than three thousand feet in contour, though in 1886 it was but 2600 feet; then Goat Island, 1300 feet wide; and finally, the American Fall, more than one thousand feet wide. But the sweep is so great that the wonderful height cannot be appreciated. The view from Prospect Point gives a better idea of height, but, because the view is in profile, the distance does not seem so much. The deficiencies of both these prospects may be corrected by a look upward from the doughty little *Maid of the Mist,* which moves back and forth over the quiet waters just below the falls.

But these are only a few of the vistas that fascinate the visitor at every turn. The rapids may be seen to wonderful advantage from the bridge that leads from the American side to Goat Island, from Terrapin Rocks, and from Three Sisters Islands. The breath-taking trip to the Cave of the Winds behind the Falls is an expedition that seems more dangerous than it is. Then the final touch is given by the twenty-mile trip on the Gorge Railroad, down the American side, to Lewiston, then up the Canadian side, three hundred feet above the Whirlpool, where it has been calculated the waters move at forty miles per hour, and on until the vista of both Falls bursts on the eye that is able to appreciate them better because of the previous studies from above and from below.

In 1835 two travelers from Scotland foresaw the day when thousands would seek the Falls, and they wrote an account of the trip in which they declared, "Niagara should be deemed the property of civilized mankind." Fifty years passed before the legislature of New York State was persuaded that they were right; then they bought the land along the American shore, as well as Goat Island—which has been called "the most beautiful island in the world." It is easy to question that judgment until the island has been visited—in summer, when the foliage submerges the visitor in varied splendor; in winter, when every twig is glorious with ice that, when the sun shines, becomes a resplendent prism. The island's plebeian name tells of the time in 1770 when it was the home of goats.

Long before the days of the goats there was a visitor on the stream opposite Goat Island that was prophet of many successors whose coming was looked on with foreboding. That visitor was a sawmill, built to prepare lumber for the erection of Fort Niagara. From that time there was talk of the frightful waste of power that might be made to do something useful. But not until 1853 were decisive steps taken to build the Hydraulic Canal on the American side. In 1885 came the first wheel-pits program, and in 1886 followed the Niagara Falls Power Company. Then so rapid was the increase of the demands on the water that the cries of those who declared the Falls would be ruined were insistent and despairing. It became popular to write articles on "The Waning Glory of Niagara,"

to tell of "Niagara Spoiled," to plead, "Hands
Off Niagara," to speak of the necessity of "Repairing
Niagara Falls," to give warning of the day when men
would begin "To Dole Out Niagara Power." One
Cassandra declared that "those who wish to see Niagara Falls in anything like their pristine beauty and
grandeur must not delay their visit very long." In
an engineering journal a paragrapher moaned, "Niagara Falls are doomed. Children already born may
yet walk dryshod from the mainland of the New York
Reservation to Goat Island, across the present bed
of the Niagara River."

But protection became effective. The United States
and Canada have agreed to guard the beauty of the
Falls. Vast power plants are still cared for, but in
such a way that Niagara persists and will continue to
give satisfaction that varies with the ideals of those
who seek its wonders. Artists and geologists, authors
and educators, men and women of world fame and
people of no fame at all, are there lost in amazement.
Some say they like to go there because, in the midst of
the tumult of the waters,there is a silence most impressive; others have declared that to them the sound of
the great cataract is a majestic harmony; as one
musician said, "the musical tone of the Falls is clear,
definite and unapproachable in its majestic perfection,
a complete series of notes, all uniting in grand and
noble accord."

CHAPTER XX

DOWN THE NEW JERSEY COAST

SOMETIMES state lines are most arbitrary. An instance is the beginning of the coast of New Jersey. In early days it was felt by many that the journey should begin at Staten Island. But they soon had to revise their notion, for word came from England that all islands in New York Bay that "could be circumnavigated in a day should belong to the province of New York." As a New York champion succeeded through his seamanship in sailing around Staten Island in the required time, the status of the island was fixed.

So the real beginning of the coast tour is on the shores of Raritan Bay and Sandy Hook Bay, with Sandy Hook reaching out a narrow finger toward Long Island. Between the finger and Long Island the endless procession of steamships and sailing vessels moves on toward New York.

The first lighthouse on Sandy Hook was built in 1762, though the land was not acquired by the government until 1816. It was bought from the heirs of Richard Hartshorn, whose name is attached to a curious document, dated 8th August, 1678. It told of the pretense of the Indians that when they sold all the land on Sandy Hook, they did not give up the right to go on Sandy Hook "to get plumbs [beach plums] when they pleased, and to hunt upon the land, and to take any tree that suited them for cannows." Then the

178

document related how, "for peace and quietness' sake," he paid thirteen shillings to Vowavapon, "to sell all rights to plumbing, hunting, fowling, fishing, getting cannows."

The region was especially attractive to the Indians because of the hills that come down to the waters of Sandy Hook Bay. These hills, known to the successors of the Indians as the Navesink Highlands, border the ocean for a distance of five miles, and rise to a height of nearly three hundred feet.

In Monmouth County, whose northen point is Sandy Hook, the sandy beach is separated from the mainland by a tidal marsh from one to six miles wide. This separating marshland is a feature of the entire coast of more than one hundred miles from Sandy Hook to Cape May. Sometimes a long narrow bay helps to remove the beach from the mainland, and here and there is a tidal inlet that adds to the picturesqueness and the extent of the coast. The first of these inlets is the Shrewsbury River which, at Red Bank, is nearly a mile wide.

These inlets may be attractive to fishermen and fair-weather sailors, but they are deadly to mariners The entire coast could tell sad stories of wrecks and glad stories of heroism of the men of the United States Life Saving Service who are grouped at short intervals where there is greatest danger.

Storms have been disastrous to Long Branch, where a hotel was built as early as 1792. At that time the place was known only as Shrewsbury. Fourteen years later there was a hotel that could accommodate more than two hundred people. In 1819 *Niles' Register* said:

"There is a kind of regulation there which strangers often contravene from ignorance, that is, when the stipulated time for ladies' bathing arrives, a white flag is hoisted on the bank, when it is high treason for gentlemen to be seen there, and when the established time for gentlemen arrives, the red flag is run up."

Long Branch was at the height of its prosperity during the Civil War and for a few years afterward. At one time homes in the vicinity were owned by George W. Childs, William E. Drexel, Edwin Booth, Lester Wallack, Maggie Mitchell, Mary Anderson, and Lily Langtry. When General Grant was President, he sometimes went to Long Branch in summer. Elberon, a short distance south, was the scene of President Garfield's gallant struggle for life in 1884.

For twenty-five miles below Long Branch beach resorts follow one another in rapid succession. Among the best known are Asbury Park, with its three freshwater lakes and its hills rising abruptly several miles back—resorts in old days of robbers who preyed on the farmers—and Ocean Grove, developed through camp-meeting activities, and luring thousands of visitors who like to go where there are no mosquitoes, and where the crowds are not too great.

Many people know the pleasures of resting by the sea when it is in its calmer mood. But unless they return in the winter season, during a time of distressing storm, they really know little of the moods of the sea. Infrequently, however, even the summer visitor gets a hint of what a winter storm can be. One August night, at Asbury Park, the roar of the breakers as they dashed on the boardwalk was like thunder. Toward morning the roar grew louder. Terrified guests—not only women, but men—came hurrying from their rooms. In a little while the parlor was filled with a company in strange array, and the clerk found his hands full as he sought to allay the fears of grown folks. There was no need to say anything to the children; they were enjoying the excitement.

South of Asbury Park, begins a forty-mile section where most of the seaside resorts are on the slender Island Beach and Long Beach, separated from the mainland by Barnegat Bay and Little Egg Harbor. From Barnegat Bay inlets lead to various resorts on the mainland, like Tom's River, noted today for its fishing as it was noted in Revolutionary times because of the resistance given to the invading British by the commander of a stone blockhouse. At length the commander was captured and hung by the enemy; but his fame has not been dimmed by his fate.

The original name of Barnegat was Barendegat, Dutch for "broken waters." The evil fame of these waters among mariners early made necessary the location of a lighthouse at the inlet to Barnegat Bay. Twenty-five years later, in 1858, a second lighthouse was built; the first had been destroyed by the encroachments of the sea. This light still stands, one hundred and sixty-five feet high. Its beams send messages of warning and assurances of safety for forty-four miles along the shore, to the heart of Highland Light on the north and Absecon Light at Atlantic City on the south. But this effective light is endangered by the encroachments of the sea, which there eats away fifteen feet of land each year. The structure was long preserved by the building of jetties that have succeeded in winning from the sea new protecting deposits of sand, but a new light may become a necessity.

Below Long Beach two inlets intervene before Atlantic City is reached—New Inlet and Absecon Inlet. Then comes the narrow island on which is built the world's most popular seaside resort, where miles of gentle sloping beach, lined by eight miles of boardwalk, provide relaxation for the tens of thousands of gay vacation-seekers who pour out from princely hotels, as well as from more modest caravanseries, and from cottages by the thousand.

It is difficult for those who, approaching Atlantic City across the marshes from Pleasantville, see the long line of the hostelries that shelter so many people, to realize that the time is comparatively short since Atlantic City put off its swaddling clothes.

In 1734 a "Gentleman" of Egg Harbor willed "Absecond Beach" to his three sons. Evidently he thought there was value in the strip of sand ten miles long, and from one-half to three-fourths of a mile wide.

Not until 1783 was the island settled. Jacob Leeds, who then owned most of the land, was the first inhabitant. On his farm was a cave, in which deserters found refuge in the Revolution, as later in the War of 1812.

In early days trips were made by people from Philadelphia and the towns between to the Absecond bathing beach. "Beach Parties," these pilgrimages were called. At first there were no bath-houses; the bather was content to dress among the sand hills. Later bath-houses were built of brush, but without a roof. The first frame bath-house was a converted wreck.

As early as 1820 the building of a resort on the

LOOKING UP THE BOARDWALK TOWARD THE STEEL PIER, ATLANTIC CITY, NEW JERSEY

ON THE BEACH AT CAPE MAY, NEW JERSEY

island was talked of. Dr. Jonathan R. Pitney, a physician, used to stroll among the sand-hills on the beach. Soon he surprised his friends by talking of a railroad from Philadelphia. The idea seemed absurd; how could a railroad through the pine barrens, with a terminus on a sand spit, be made to pay?

At this time a visitor spoke of Absecon Island as "a rough looking place, the sandhills being covered with course, stunted grass, mixed with trees. There were only two boarding houses. Some of the best land was offered at $17.50 per acre."

"And most of that same land is now worth one dollar per front foot!" wrote an astonished man in 1883. He would have been an unbeliever if he had been told of the fabulous prices paid for beach property a generation later.

The railroad from Philadelphia was chartered in 1852. Then a name was desired for the new resort on Absecon. Ocean City, Seabeach, Surfing, Strand, and Bath were among other names suggested. When Dr. Pitney presented to the Board of Directors of the railroad the plot of the proposed bathing place, they noted the name Atlantic City written on it.

The first excursion was run on July 1, 1854, when there were six hundred passengers!

Modern excursionists take pleasure in the journey by motor-boat along the waters back of Atlantic City, down to Great Egg Harbor and Ocean City. There they are on water made famous during the Revolution by the exploits of privateers who lay in wait for prizes between the Harbor and Cape May. One of these privateers was an open boat called *The Skunk*, with two guns and twelve men, which took nine prizes in a short time.

Cape May, the southern limit of the excursions of this privateer, which also marks the southern boundary of what has been called "the world's greatest playground," was named for Captain Cornelius Mey, first director of the New Netherlands, who, in 1623, sailed south on a trip of exploration. When he reached the entrance to Delaware Bay, he gave his name to the north cape. Modestly, however, he called the south cape Cornelius. This meant self-denial, for he had called New York Port Mey, and the Delaware New Port Mey. All the names have been changed, except that of the north cape.

In 1630 Skipper Peter Heyssen bought from the Indians a tract of land four miles long on the bay from Cape May to the north, and extending five miles inland. At once he made the region a whaling ground. In 1633, in a single day, seven whales were caught near by.

In 1641 Sweden bought Cape May, and in 1664 the English were in control. During the Revolution Cape May became well known, not only because of the privateers, but because of the clams which the inhabitants boiled out, dried and strung for transportation to the patriot army.

In 1812 the first Congress Hall was built on what was then known as Cape Island. Other hotels followed. In 1845 it was said that "three thousand strangers annually visit the place, which is separated by a small creek from the mainland."

For many years before the Civil War the resort at the southern limit of New Jersey was popular with

184

ON TOMS RIVER, NEW JERSEY

people from the South as well as from the North. Later its popularity was temporarily eclipsed by other resorts, but now Cape May has resumed its proper place, luring by the thousand visitors who have learned that, when once they seek the Cape, they are tempted to return year after year to the spot where modest Captain Mey showed the way nearly three hundred years ago.

CHAPTER XXI

THE VIVID CONTRASTS OF NEW JERSEY

A COMPANY of travelers in a railway coach were comparing notes about New Jersey. One of them, with the assurance frequently shown by those whose experience has been more or less limited, declared emphatically:

"New Jersey is the most monotonous state in the East. I have crossed it a dozen times, and have always found the experience so dreary that I have dreaded to repeat it. Sand and scrub pines are not a pleasant program on the road."

A second traveler whose experience had been just as limited put in his word:

"I have found miles of rough, hilly traveling in New Jersey, and I advise automobile owners to avoid that state if they can. It is true, there are many good roads, but the grades are often heavy, and the difficulties are many."

"I, too, have driven across New Jersey many times," said a third man, "but I have not found it monotonous, and I have not been disturbed by the pines. To me it seems a very commonplace bit of country, not in any respect different from that encountered a dozen times in the course of a journey from New York to St. Louis—that is, except for the broad marshes that must be crossed before it is possible to reach the ferries to New York City."

186

CRANBERRY BOG, WEST OF MT. PLEASANT, NEW JERSEY

IN THE PINE BARRENS OF NEW JERSEY

IN THE PINES, LAKEWOOD, NEW JERSEY

THE VIVID CONTRASTS OF NEW JERSEY

Now one of those men had traversed the wonderful Pine Barrens south of the center of the state, in the neighborhood of the Mullica River—a region of fifteen hundred square miles where the plant growth is so abundant and so varied that this is a favorite hunting ground for botanists; where there is so much evidence that this part of the state was once an island in the ocean that geologists find it pleasant to go there; where there are so many bits like parts of Nantucket that those who favor the Massachusetts island have learned the joys of walking trips in this abode of peace so much nearer home; where the hunter may find deer in satisfying numbers and the photographers may see them feeding on some of the scrub that to some is so uninviting; where there is an acre of trees in whose tops is a blue heronry that makes the ornithologist leap for joy. Many lovers of the wild are eager to have a portion of these Pine Barrens set apart as a State Reserve; they long to see preserved for future generations beauties that are so different from anything else on the lower Atlantic Coast that they have attracted to Lakewood, in the upper corner of the region of pines, builders of stately homes as well as seekers for health and pleasure who delight to listen to the wind in the tree tops or to wander beside Lake Carasaljo, that momento of a father's impartial desire to commemorate the fame of his daughters Carrie, Sallie, and Josephine.

The route of the man who had found mountains and difficult grades in his crossing of New Jersey, was in the north, where the Kittatinny Mountain comes down to the Delaware, bowing low at the Water Gap to permit the river to rush through. He probably passed within hailing distance of that point in the Blue

Mountains called the Indian Ladder, where the Indians by a rude tree ladder ascended the difficult precipice that hindered access to the country back from the river, and where the first white settlers used a rope ladder for the like purpose. He had, no doubt, seen Greenwood Lake, in its setting in the hills, half in New Jersey, half in New York, and perhaps he had passed along the shore of winding Lake Hopatcong, which was called "the great pond" in an advertisement of lands to be sold at public vendue in 1757. When he passed through a country that is like a bit of the heart of North Carolina, with its heights and valleys, its river gorges cut through the trap rock, its cascades and falls like those which furnish both beauty and water power at Paterson and Passaic. Its crowning feature, in the opinion of many, is that matchless trap ridge, the Palisades, which for twenty-five miles marks the western bank of the Hudson River. This was a favorite country with the Indians. Through it the pioneer sought the Poconos, and the Moravians went to the Delaware, while Washington and his colonial troops marched and countermarched there, between the Delaware, a strategic barrier in a number of campaigns, Morristown, which still proudly shows the General's Headquarters, and the Hudson River, where Fort Lee long bade defiance to the British.

The third man who that day on the railway expressed his rather unfavorable opinion of New Jersey scenery crossed one of the most delightful sections of a state which includes such infinite variety that those who know the region best sometimes wonder if it is possible to find more of interest and appeal in any other eight thousand square miles of the country's area. He

188

crossed the state by another route that was a favorite
path in colonial days and in the Revolution, beginning
the journey close to the boundary between the lands
of Lord Berkeley and those of Lord Carteret—the
East and West sections of the Province of New Jersey.
He probably crossed the Delaware at Trenton Falls,
scene of the fishing party in 1767 when Benjamin
Franklin and Governor Banning Wentworth of New
Hampshire watched their lines and swapped yarns.
He was then near the spot that, in 1784 and for some
years later was seriously considered by Congress as
a site for the permanent capital of the United States.
He went to Trenton, scene of Washington's famous
victory over the British and of that later engagement
named by a writer of the time "the cannonade at Trent
Town." William Trent, who gave his name to the
town, and later became Chief Justice of the Supreme
Court of the Province, which had its session there,
surely would have been astonished if he could have seen
the modern city with its dominating gilt dome of
the capitol.

From Trenton to Princeton the route is not only
of great charm but is also full of historic memories.
Those miles were stubbornly contested by the rival
forces of the Crown and the Colonies. Lawrenceville,
named for the naval hero who pleaded with his men,
"Don't Give up the Ship," was known as Maidenhead
to the troops who passed that way, some of them to
the Battle of Princeton. The ridge road between
Lawrenceville and Princeton crosses Stony Brook
within a short distance of the site of the battle, "which
in the short space of half an hour, decided the fate of

189

the United States," and near by is the house—still standing—where General Mercer died.

That ride from Lawrenceville to Princeton, with its view to the lowlands north and south, is anything but commonplace. It passes through rolling meadows and green woodlands which seem to say, "Linger with us," and it leads to a town which combines the charm of an English university village and the freshness and vigor of an American educational center. From the Graduate College, whose graceful tower rises high above the trees and is reflected in the mirror of the water close at hand, to the elm-shaded campus, where the central feature is Nassau Hall, the town is a dream of beauty.

The story of Nassau Hall, marvel of the colonies, is told in a tablet near the entrance door:

"This building, erected in 1756 by the college of New Jersey, and named Nassau Hall in honor of King William III, was seized by British forces for military purposes in 1776, and retaken by the American Army January 3, 1777. Here Congress met from June 30, 1783, until November 4, 1783, and here, August 20, 1783, General Washington received the grateful acknowledgments of the Congress for his service in establishing the freedom and independence of the United States of America."

And in this historic building, at the commencement of 1783, Ashbel Green, the Valedictorian, turned to General Washington, and made his prophecy of the days when the deeds of the patriots should be told:

"Never in that day, illustrious and magnanimous chief, shall thy actions and thy exploits be unrecorded. Some future bard, whom all the muses love—oh, that

FORD MANSION, MORRISTOWN, NEW JERSEY
Washington's Headquarters

THE GRADUATE COLLEGE, PRINCETON, NEW JERSEY

ON THE RARITAN RIVER, NEW JERSEY

it might be some happy son of Nassau Hall!—shall
tell in all the majesty of epic song, the man whose
prudent conduct, and whose gallant sword, taught the
tyrants of the earth to fear oppression, and opened an
asylum for the virtuous, free to all the world. But—
adventurous bard, whoever thou art, beware! Leave
poetic fiction and ornament to those whose theme requires it; the greatest panegyric of my hero is his
true character."

"The War Path of the Revolution" leads on from
Princeton, close to the waters of the Delaware and
Raritan Canal, which was constructed more than a
generation after the close of the Revolution, and within
view of the distant ridge of hills that dips gracefully
to the valley near Bound Brook, making place for the
rugged country whose central feature is Chimney Rock
favorite resort of the residents of Plainfield.

Past Bound Brook from the northwest flows the
winding Raritan—called by a traveler of 1775 the Ra-
rington. On the banks of this, the largest river
altogether within New Jersey, at picturesque New
Brunswick, ancient Rutgers College has its seat. From
there the stream flows smoothly on, soon widening for
its entrance to Raritan Bay, to Perth Amboy, called
Perth Town by the Proprietor of New Jersey, who
planned a settlement which should be "the most con-
siderable in these parts." New York soon distanced
Perth Town in importance, but the settlement on Ambo
Point became the seat of the Proprietor's Government,
as it was later the capital of the royal province.

From the Raritan at New Brunswick the old route
across this charming section of New Jersey passes on

to Elizabeth, famous from colonial days, and to Newark, the splendid manufacturing city that stands between the highlands that look to the interior and the marshlands that look toward New York City. These Hackensack marshes—a "glacial scoop," the geologist calls them—crossed in many directions by highways and railroads bound for the city by the Hudson, are of perennial interest. Many who traverse them daily never weary of the stretch that to others seem monotonous. The varied vegetation of catkins and reed grasses, wind-blown, dipped in the waters of the tide, the intersecting tidal creeks, the lonely cabins of fishermen and the masts of catboats, combine to make a picture of agreeable flatness, surprisingly relieved by rocky Snake Hill, which was the central feature of Mount Pinhorne, the estate of William Pinhorne, retired statesman from the growing town across the tide.

And nothing has been said of Paterson, which Alexander Hamilton tried vainly to develop as a manufacturing center, only to be compelled to leave the opportunity for later and more successful men; of that group of suburbs near Newark that invite the city dweller to the shadow of the hill and the music of the stream; of Phillipsburg, from the brow of a hill commanding the Delaware where it is at the best; of Salem, where the English attempted a settlement in 1841; of Camden, the home of Walt Whitman, a city which deserves to receive more attention than is given to it by visitors to the larger city across the Delaware; of Bordentown, long the retreat of Joseph Bonaparte in his exile; of Cranbury, where David Brainerd preached to the Indians; of Freehold, where the battle of Monmouth Court House was fought with the British; of Vineland, whose grove to those who died in the Great War has been called by the American Forestry Association "the most unique natural monument in the United States;" of scores of other towns and cities whose names have deserved a place in the annals of the artist, the historian and the tourist.

CHAPTER XXII

ON DELAWARE'S WESTERN SHORE

HOW did Delaware happen? The question comes spontaneously to those who look at its curious boundaries and slender proportions, from the circular northern line which takes an inconvenient bite out of Pennsylvania, to the southwestern right angle that is such an inconsequential stopping place. Why doesn't the boundary go on at least as far as the present southern line of Maryland? What is the logic of the line that bisects the peninsula between Delaware Bay and Chesapeake Bay?

There is nothing logical in Delaware's boundaries. But there is romantic history behind every line, history that tells of the Swedes and the Dutch and the English; of jealousy between Proprietors and of conflicting grants from the English Crown; of the desire of the Duke of York that William Penn should have control of the navigation of the Delaware; of endless disputes and compromises. The last of these disputes was not finally settled until 1889, when a Joint Commission from Maryland and Delaware drew a curve from the spire of New Castle Courthouse, with a radius of twelve miles, marking the northern boundary. Even this action was a compromise; for it was found that a true arc would take from Delaware land which she had cherished as her own for nearly two hundred years. So a compound curve brought the solution of a difficulty that had continued since 1701.

194

ON DELAWARE'S WESTERN SHORE

There is within the circular boundary line so much of charming hill and dale that the wanderer afield begins to wonder if that line was not drawn by a lover of nature, a kindred spirit of Bayard Taylor, who delighted to take jaunts from his home just over the Pennsylvania line to the streams and the hills of the country northeast of Wilmington. He never wearied of the landscape in the Hockessin Valley, and those who follow in his footsteps will not need to question why.

There are hills and woodlands in the north, and there are swift streams that supply abundant water power. Farther south there are more sluggish streams as well as much tidal marshland. In the extreme south there is a cypress swamp more than seventy square miles in extent. Along the streams and in the valleys are scenes that make the visitor from England think of some of the best of the rural scenery of that country. Early English residents left evidences of their appreciation of this fact in the names they gave to the three counties of Delaware: New Castle, Kent and Sussex. The town that was to become the capital they called Dover, and the primary political divisions they called hundreds instead of townships.

History as well as scenery begin as soon as the state is entered from the north. On the Delaware, a little below the boundary line, is Grubb's Landing, now a memory, but in colonial days a shipping point of importance. During the Revolution the British found it a favorable landing place for sloops.

Not far away there is a creek—Naaman's Creek—that flows down toward the bay after passing a house that dates from the coming of the Swedes, with a block-house near by that was built in 1654. Close to the house was, until recently, an old bridge erected in 1802, on the site of an earlier bridge over which Washington passed with his army in 1777, when on his way to intercept the British. The development of the region for manufacturing purposes during the Great War threatened the existence of these old landmarks; passengers on the railroad and tourists who crossed the bridge on the way to Washington thought regretfully of the time when this glory of historic Delaware may be sacrificed.

But, fortunately, there is a spirit in Delaware that leads to strenuous efforts to save such survivals as those at Naaman's Creek. Witness the protests made in Wilmington to protect the quaint structure of the First Presbyterian Church, built in 1740, whose site was coveted, since it was in the heart of the business district. The problem was finally solved when the Delaware Societies of the Colonial Dames and the Colonial Wars arranged for the removal of the brick structure to Brandywine Drive.

Wilmington, long called Willington, has been spoken of as the Plymouth Rock of Delaware, for the city marks the site where the Swedes, attracted by the hills, first landed. It has been said of the city that it is "as full of lumps as a napkin thrown over a blackberry bush." In 1638 the Swedes and Finns erected Fort Christiana near the mouth of the Christiana Creek.

Wilmington has not only Christiana Creek, but it has the Brandywine, which was valued for its water power even in 1729, when there were two mills near the mouth of the stream. In 1764 there were eight mills. In colonial days these were the main dependence of Washington's army for wheat. Then, for fear they

IN COOL SPRING PARK, WILMINGTON, DELAWARE

THE OLD RODNEY HOUSE NEAR DOVER, DELAWARE
(The Rear Wing is the Original House)

READ HOUSE, NEW CASTLE, DELAWARE
From the Garden

would be of like use to the British, Washington ordered that they be dismantled, as soon as he heard of the landing of the army of the enemy at the Head of Elk on the Chesapeake, so near at hand.

The landing of the British led to another historic incident. On Sept. 3, 1777, the outposts of the Colonial army and the advance guard of the British army clashed at Cooch's Bridge, on Little Christiana, six miles below Wilmington. During this skirmish the Stars and Stripes were first unfurled in battle. A monument near the site of Cooch's Bridge tells the story.

A short trip from Cooch's Bridge brings the traveler to New Castle, an old-world town, on the banks of the Delaware, at a point where the stream widens perceptibly in its majestic advance to the sea. Here the Dutch built Fort Casimir in 1651. The town followed in 1655; two years later it was called New Amstel. Then 167 people came from Amsterdam to settle there, relying on the promise of the mother city to give them passage across the ocean, lay out the town, and supply a schoolmaster.

Max Adeler called New Castle "the only finished town in America." It is a beautiful place, with its old trees, its village Green, its wealth of colonial houses which show a bewildering variety of entrance doors and other equally charming features, its surviving Dutch house on the Green, the court-house, part of it built in 1676, and its ancient Episcopal and Presbyterian churches.

Neighbor to the ancient churches of New Castle was the near-by Pencader church, in Pencader Hundred, organized in 1710, which took its name from the title given by the Welsh settlers to Iron Hill, the "highest seat." In early days iron was mined in the hill.

To the north of Iron Hill is Newark, the ancient town has been famous for educational institutions since the organization there, in 1767, of the Newark Academy, which survived for many years after Delaware College, now the University of Delaware, was established. The white-columned buildings of the college are a striking feature of the street that was long, the only street of the town. At one time this street inspired a schoolboy to write: "Newark has for fifty years been increasing at both ends, and, should this increase continue, owing to the rotundity of the earth, the two ends will in the course of a few thousand years meet."

The people of Newark were interested as early as 1767 in a project to dig a canal from the Delaware to the Chesapeake. Early surveys called for a canal that would have passed close to Newark. The first attempt, begun in 1804, was a failure in spite of the fact that Benjamin H. Latrobe, later the architect of the Capitol at Washington, was in charge of construction. The money subscribed was exhausted in building a reservoir to be fed from Elk River.

The Delaware and Chesapeake Canal was finally completed, a little farther south, in 1829. The beginning of the thirteen-mile course is at Delaware City, which was called Newbold's Landing until the prospect of the coming of the canal led to the booming of a new town and the building of ten houses—an achievement celebrated by the feeding of all comers at an immense table in the street a full block long.

It is remarkable that when, in 1907, a commission appointed by the President to recommend a route from

198

the Chesapeake to the Delaware, the old canal was named, in accordance with the word of a far-sighted man who, in 1804, spoke of this canal as "a possible link of interior communication along the coasts of the United States, which has often been contemplated."

There were towns in Delaware that did not wait for canals to take advantage of the little streams that led to the Delaware. One of these was Cantwell's Bridge, so called because of a tollbridge over a little stream that was deep enough to carry a goodly commerce. In 1825 the town was a shipping point of note. Granaries were built on the banks of the stream, and grain for shipment was brought from points many miles around. In 1855 the grain trade was such an important element in the town's prosperity that the citizens changed the name to Odessa, in the proud belief that this port was worthy to be classed with Odessa, on the Black Sea. Almost at once, however, pride had a fall; the railroad passed that way, and Odessa, confident in her water facilities, refused to give it needed encouragement. The track was built to the westward, Middletown soon sprang up, and the prosperity of Odessa became a memory.

Names from the Near East were almost as popular in early Delaware as names of places in England. To the south of Odessa is a town known originally as Duck Creek Cross Roads, though later it became Smyrna.

Between Smyrna and the Delaware is a decayed village, Wapping, whose first settlers evidently thought with longing of the section of London of that name. More fortunate than they were those who chose the English name Dover for the town that, in 1777, became the capital of Delaware.

Dover is like a bit of Kent in England. Here, too, there is a central Green. On this fronts the old State House, which dates from 1787. Near at hand is the ancient whipping-post. This post stood on that day in 1776 when Cæsar Rodney led the citizens who took the portrait of George III from the courthouse and burned it on the Green.

Dover has another claim to fame. Past there to the Delaware flows the St. Jones River, which might well be called Snake River; the distance as a bird flies is but eight miles, but the tortuous course of the stream is seventeen miles. For more than a century the farmers of the vicinity have been talking of straightening the crooked river, which is navigable for small steamers.

Streams in Delaware are noted for other things than crooks and turns. Some of them have names as crooked as their courses. There is the Appoquinnimink, near Glasgow, and there is the Mispillion, on whose banks Milford was founded in 1680, close to the holdings of merchants from Barbadoes who were taking part in a land speculation in Milford Hundred.

A few miles beyond the mouth of the Mispillion, Delaware Bay, which receives its waters, gives way to the broad Atlantic. Near the point that looks up toward the Delaware River, and out on the ocean, Lewes has its site. The town was a little fishing hamlet when it won lasting fame in 1813. On April 6 of that year a British blockading fleet arrived off the town. The commander needed provisions. It did not occur to him that it would be necessary to do more than make his desire known. Did he not have plenty of guns? So he wrote to the town's first magistrate, stating his wants, and saying, "If you refuse to comply, I shall be under the necessity of destroying your town."

Yet the doughty "first magistrate" sent word to the governor, who went to Lewes and encouraged it in its defence. The legislature appropriated $2000 for the expense of the game of bluff the town was playing. The town possessed only two eighteen-pounders, though there were no ball for them. There were two nine-pounders, but the ball provided for these were too large. And there were but fifteen casks of powder.

The attack began. The result must have punctured the pride of the British commander. For as fast as he fired balls ashore, they were picked up and fired back.

The damage inflicted on the town was but two thousand dollars. As the local wag said:

> "The Commander and all his men
> Shot a dog and killed a hen."

After twenty-two hours cannonading, the fleet withdrew—five launches, two sloops, a motor boat, a pilot boat, a schooner and a frigate!

Today Lewes is known to navigation because of the Delaware Breakwater, begun in 1818, and the Harbor of Refuge, built between 1897 and 1911, where storm-tossed ships seek safety in the protected anchorage.

CHAPTER XXIII

PHILADELPHIA, BIRTHPLACE OF THE NATION

THERE is a garden in Philadelphia where visitors are shown a series of remarkable stepping stones. One stone was brought from the scene of the battle of Germantown, while its neighbor came from historic Brandywine. Other stones were found on General Wolfe's pathway to the Plains of Abraham at Quebec; on the site of America's first paper mill, built by William Rittenhouse, close to the banks of the Wissahickon; and at Washington's Headquarters at Chadds Ford. The homes of William Penn and Anthony Wayne likewise contributed to the storied pathway, while Valley Forge helped to complete the remarkable series of stepping stones.

But Philadelphia offers to visitors a far more remarkable and satisfactory pathway than that in the garden of the historian—more remarkable because it speaks with greater eloquence of history; more satisfactory because it is marked not merely by bits of stones associated with great events, but by the sites and frequently the shrines where history was made. Each year this pathway is trodden reverently by tens of thousands of pilgrims who find in the square mile of territory between Philadelphia's rivers, in the heart of the city, one of the world's most remarkable nests of antiquities. An afternoon's jaunt is ample for a hasty tour past these memorials of a glorious past,

202

THE PARKWAY, PHILADELPHIA, SCHUYLKILL RIVER AND
FAIRMOUNT PARK IN THE DISTANCE
(From the Tower of the City Hall)

INDEPENDENCE HALL, LOOKING TOWARD CONGRESS HALL, PHILADELPHIA

but many afternoons may well be filled with inspection of the buildings that still triumph over the genius for destruction which has laid low so many priceless relics of the days gone by.

Down near the Delaware quaint Old Swedes Church speaks of the days of 1700, while not far away St. Peter's Church and Old Pine Street Church, relics of Revolutionary times, stand with august dignity among the clustering gravestones. Within a short distance Carpenters Hall, meeting place of the first Continental Congress, peeps out from its hiding place amid the tall structures of commerce. Less than two squares distant the most glorious structure in America, Independence Hall, looks down with quiet dignity on crowded Chestnut Street and the quaint "State House Yard" that can never quite lose its touch with the days of the past when the Declaration of Independence was read from a scaffolding erected there by the Philosophic Society for the convenience of those who would observe the Transit of Venus. From the yard the door opens invitingly on the mute Liberty Bell, resting in its glass case where all can read the prophetic inscription and see the great crack which iconoclasts have proposed to heal by electric welding. And up the stairs, above the bell, are the priceless relics of Washington and of Congress, as well as the portraits of the Signers and other men thought worthy to keep company with them. Step softly there, and linger quietly in the halls where walked the intrepid men who gave America a place among the nations!

By the side of Independence Hall is Congress Hall, the Capitol of the United States from 1790 to 1800, where Washington was inaugurated in 1793, and where later he read his Farewell Address. Only three squares distant is the first United States Bank, built in 1797, while it is but a short distance to Christ Church, built in 1727. There the great street window shares attention with the tomb of Robert Morris in the churchyard and the pews of George Washington and Betsy Ross.

The house of Betsy Ross where—so it is claimed— the first American flag was made, is within a stone's throw of Christ Church, while less than three squares farther on is the old graveyard where Benjamin Franklin was buried. Old Quaker meeting houses are near neighbors of the Colonial Philosopher's grave, while a little to the south, on Market street, are marked the sites of George Washington's residence in Philadelphia when he was President, and the house where Thomas Jefferson drafted the Declaration of Independence.

The next halting place in the historic pathway is at the Post Office, where the statue of Benjamin Franklin marks what is supposed to be the place where he flew the kite that put him on speaking terms with electricity. From there it is but ten minutes' walk to the building of the Library Company of Philadelphia, founded by Franklin in 1731, the first circulating library in America. William Penn's desk and clock and Franklin's electric machine repose within the walls that are near neighbors to the Historical Society of Pennsylvania, with its remarkable collection of relics, including the wampum belt given to William Penn by the Indians; George Washington's desk, used when he was President; John Paul Jones' sword; Anthony Wayne's sword; Abraham Lincoln's office furniture and law books; and the autograph manuscripts of the "Star-

CHRIST CHURCH, PHILADELPHIA
Where Washington went to Church
Erected 1727; tower built in 1752

WASHINGTON'S HEADQUARTERS, VALLEY FORGE, PENNSYLVANIA

THE WASHINGTON MEMORIAL CHAPEL, VALLEY FORGE, PENNSYLVANIA

Spangled Banner, "Home. Sweet Home," and "Hail Columbia."

Now is a good time to pass to the City Hall, built on the site of the camp the army of Washington and Rochambeau made on the way to Yorktown in 1781. The central feature of the building is the great tower, surmounted by the statue of William Penn, whose hat is 548 feet high. An elevator whisks the visitor to the base of the statue, where he can look out on Old Philadelphia, marveling at the neighborliness of all that he has seen; over to West Philadelphia, where locomotives once waited for freight cars drawn by mules and passenger cars drawn by more mules from the Delaware River to the region across the Schuylkill; down the Delaware to its confluence with the Schuylkill, where is located the country's greatest naval station, League Island; up the Delaware, where modern vessels travel unconsciously in the pathway of John Fitch's first steamboat experiments; up the Schuylkill toward Germantown, with its memorials of the Revolution, and Chestnut Hill, the beautiful; out the great Parkway, that leads from the heart of the city to wonderful Fairmount, the largest park in the world, with its famous Wissahickon Drive, where a brawling stream leaps between leafy banks far down in a gorge that might be in the heart of a wilderness instead of within a great city; and, finally, on to the wooded hills and valleys to the west, where cluster some of America's loveliest suburbs, paving the way to Valley Forge, where Washington's heroes endured the dreadful winter of 1777-1778.

There, in the midst of a gloriously beautiful natural park, the Headquarters of Washington are preserved, as well as the old entrenchments, and the replica of one of the log huts in which the soldiers lived, built according to specifications laid down in records of long ago.

But the greatest feature of the park by the Schuyl-kill is the Washington Memorial Chapel, whose Gothic walls and marvelous windows provide fit enclosure for the memorials of the great leader who inspired his men with the patriotic devotion that led three thousand of them to yield their lives during the storms of that dreadful winter, and other thousands who survived to risk their lives in the campaigns that followed.

The Memorial Chapel is the central feature of the park, and the central feature of the chapel is the altar on whose steps have been cut the lines of Tennyson:

> His work is done;
> But while the race of mankind endure,
>   Let his great example stand
>   Colossal, seen of every land,
> And keep the soldier firm, the statesman pure,
>   Till in all lands, and thro' all human story,
>   The path of duty be the way of glory.

CHAPTER XXIV

AMONG THE PENNSYLVANIA MOUNTAINS

NOT only is the surface of Pennsylvania more diversified than that of any other state west of the Rockies, but it has within its borders a section of the mountains wider than that in any other state from Maine to Alabama. The Alleghenies in the central portion and an extension of the Blue Ridge from the Gettysburg region northeast to the Delaware River provide enough summits and plateaus and valleys to startle the visitor who has had the notion that the state has in it comparatively little scenic grandeur.

Yet there are summits like Blue Knob, in Bedford County, 3,136 feet high, and Big Bald Knob, on the line of Somerset and Bedford counties, around 3,000 feet above the sea. There are towns on the plateaus that are two thousand feet high and more, and there is, in the middle of the state, an area of about two thousand square miles where the barometer indicates an altitude of two thousand feet.

Geologists find these Pennsylvania highlands a field of perennial interest. The upheavals and the erosions that have shaped the mountains and the valley have exposed the rocks in fascinating fashion. Rocks that at Emporium or Driftwood in north central Pennsylvania are as much as five miles below the surface, are so near the surface in the Nittany Valley, only a short distance to the southeast, that it is there possible to study the earliest stratified rocks of the region. This is especially true near State College.

In the course of a few hour's walk above Lock Haven, on the West Branch of the Susquehanna, the stroller can examine all the rocks in succession from the Silurian to the coal measures. An even fuller disclosure awaits the pedestrian who will pass leisurely from Salona on the Bellefonte Central Railroad through the gap to Mill Hall, to Lock Haven, and from there up the river. Even the passenger on the train along this stretch of the Susquehanna will note the curious upheavals of the strata, while the man with only a rudimentary knowledge of geology may walk among these upheavals, with hammer in hand, and will uncover endless romances of the plants and animals of untold generations.

"The secret of the coal measures of Pennsylvania soon becomes an open book to such a wanderer," a Pennsylvania geologist said to the author, "for he will learn what is meant by the statement that the entire surface of the state was once overlaid with coal, and that the overlay has all disappeared in Eastern Pennsylvania except in the anthracite basin where coal went down so deep in the valleys that the process of erosion did not reach it. In Western Pennsylvania, where there was only half a mile of erosion, there is at the surface bituminous coal, which has entirely disappeared in the east."

The remarkable anthracite area is but a little over three thousand square miles. And this is the only anthracite in the country, except a little in Colorado

GIANT ANT HILLS, BEDFORD STATE FOREST, NEAR RAINSBURG, PENNSYLVANIA

BEAVER DAM, SIZERVILLE STATE FOREST, CAMERON COUNTY, PENNSYLVANIA

A WESTERN PENNSYLVANIA SOFT COAL COLLIERY

BLAIR GAP, PENNSYLVANIA

and New Mexico. There are nearly five times as many square miles of bituminous coal measures.

Many of the mountain regions of Western Pennsylvania were once illuminated by the fires of those who provided still another fuel—the tenders of the coke ovens. Melancholy ruins of thousands of these ovens which once belched fire in an astonishing manner, are to be seen by travelers along the railroads that cross the mountains. They were abandoned because of the exhaustion of the coal, in favor of new fields like those in southwestern Pennsylvania.

Many years before the immigrants passed westward to their black toil in the bowels of the earth or among the volcano-like ovens, pioneers of another race made their weary way over the mountains, most of them choosing the route that is now known as the Lincoln Highway. A reminder of their passage still stands, on the eastern slope of Chestnut Ridge, nine miles west of Bedford—an old frame church with its surrounding graves, built on the site given for the purpose by John Schell, the first settler of the region. There many of the seekers after western homes stopped to rest and worship, and a few found in the graveyard on the ridge a longer resting place for their weary bones.

When railroads were first talked of, most people declared that it was impossible to find a practicable route over the mountains in Pennsylvania; that it would be necessary to be satisfied with highways or with a railroad far to the south. As late as 1844, Pittsburgh citizens felt that, in order to reach Philadelphia by rail, they must seek a connection with the Baltimore and Ohio Railroad. Their only hope of getting to the city by the Delaware was through three states to the south. Yet few advocated the direct route. Senator Bigler, who was to become the governor of the Commonwealth, ventured to foretell improvements in construction and locomotion that would make possible a more direct route across the mountains.

His faith triumphed. The mountains were conquered, and there was provided the direct route, up the Juniata, through the gap and over the ridge to the summit near Horseshoe Curve, and then down through the valley of the Conemaugh toward the city by the Ohio.

That pioneer railroad, and its branches to the right and to the left, have shown to countless thousands some of the glories of the uplands, and have lured a comparatively few choice spirits into the hidden fastnesses, far from the railroads where, in the regions of solitary splendor, they have learned really to know the mountains.

It isn't such a simple matter to know the mountains. Real knowledge involves climbing them in June. It means listening, in July, to the green trees reaching up, up, up the slopes as they whisper to each other the secrets of the forest. It includes, in August, whipping the trout stream as it dashes down the mountain side, hastening to reach the lower lands, all unconscious that the time is coming when it will sigh in vain for return to the upper heaven-kissing slopes. In September acquaintance with the mountains means watching the leaves of the favored aristocratic trees that grow where the frost reaches them early, hastening the time of their appearance in rainbow colors, as if to anticipate the departure of the men and women and children who will soon return to their usual round for the winter.

But the boast of those who insist that they know the mountains is vain, if they have seen them only in the summer. Go to them in winter! Make friends with them in November, when the trees on the slopes lift aloft their ghostly arms and give voice in accents that are but a hoarse and sorrowful echo of their summer sighing. Abide with them in December, when thick ice locks the brooks and whirls along the bleak open spaces and among the shuddering trees, swiftly transforming the slopes into beauty that makes the beholder breathless in his wonder, clothing the nakedness of the trees until they are like great pillows, fluffed out with softest down. Then revel in their company in February, when the blanket from the skies lies everywhere so thick it seems impossible that the landscape can ever regain its well-remembered summer aspect.

The trail of the man who knows and delights in the mountains is everywhere in Pennsylvania. Follow him to Center County, where Snow Shoe hints of early visitors to remote knobs that are rugged and steep. Then far to the east in Northampton County Wind Gap —once the pathway of the majestic moose in search of southern pasturage—tells of a pioneer with the soul of a poet, who found keen joy in thinking of the ages when perhaps a stream found passage through the gap, was hindered by a hard ridge, and changed its course. So names that are eloquent become familiar to the wanderer in the Highlands of Pennsylvania, making him forget other belittling titles that have been fastened on some of the outstanding marvels of the State.

The legends that cluster about these mountains have been gathered with loving patience by Colonel Henry W. Shoemaker, whose home, Restless Oaks, near McElhattan, in Clinton County, is in the heart of the heights which are his delight. From his garden he looks across the West Branch, far off into McElhattan Gap, notable even in Pennsylvania. Close to Colonel Shoemaker's dooryard a stone tells of another Indian James Logan, the famous Mingo chief, and the old black oak tree under which he used to rest when on his way across the mountain wilderness to his favorite camp ground at the Sulphur Springs.

The journey to the springs which the Indian orator took so often leads across majestic Bald Eagle Mountain, and then through a succession of valleys buried in the heart of the Pennsylvania Highlands, to Penn's Cave, cunningly hidden deep in a leafy glen. The only entrance to the cavern is by water, for water fills all of the winding passage. Flat bottomed boats, motor driven, await those who have learned how to find their way to this gem of the Highlands. The guide who conducted the author's party through the maze had a penetrating but sympathetic voice and the slow quarter-of-a-mile journey under the vaulted roof with its curiously shaped stalactites was an object lesson in geology, for there the process of erosion that shaped the mountains and valleys of Pennsylvania during the ages is still going on.

Without warning the ride was at an end; the limestone roof descended to the water where it sinks into the foundation of the mountain, only to reappear in the open air some distance away, as Karoondinha Creek, whose source is within the cave.

PINE CREEK GORGE, LYCOMING COUNTY, PENNSYLVANIA

ENTRANCE TO PENN'S CAVE, CENTER COUNTY, PENNSYLVANIA

After visiting the cave and listening to its legend is the time to take what has been called the finest railroad ride in Pennsylvania—from Montander on the Pennsylvania Railroad above Sunbury to Bellefonte on the Lewisburg and Tyrone Railroad. The route is perhaps seventy-five miles long. But these miles are so wonderful that it seems a pity not to cover them on foot or on a horse. The route is through Buffalo Valley, then through the Tight End of Union County, following the Karoondinha from Farrandsville to Coburn. From Coburn to Spring Mill the creek is lined with virgin timber which frequently comes down to the very bank of the stream. The country has hardly changed since the time when the Indians filed through the valley, or the later time when the wheat-laden arks floated down to Harrisburg and Baltimore.

Not far from Spring Mill is the spot where the Karoondinha lost since its disappearance in Penn's Cave, issues from its depths in full-grown beauty. Of all the virgin timber in the valley of the Karoondinha—or Penn's Valley, as it is also called—the most noticeable trees at the time of the visit of the author were near Aaronsburg; they were known to the men of the State Forestry Department as the Monarch and the Three Allies, stately white pines that lifted their plumed crowns to a height of one hundred and thirty feet or more. Experts declared that the trees were from two hundred to three hundred years old.

Standing beneath these giants, and looking far up the great trunks, it seems natural to think of the song of Henry van Dyke:

"I will sing of the bounty of the big trees,
They are the green tents of the Almighty,
He hath set them up for comfort and for shelter.

"Their cords hath he knotted in the earth,
He hath driven their stakes securely,
Their roots take hold of the rocks like iron.

"He sendeth into their bodies the sap of life,
They lift themselves lightly toward the heavens;
They rejoice in the broadening of their branches.

"Their leaves drink in the sunlight and the air,
They talk softly together when the breeze bloweth,
Their shadow in the noon-day is full of coolness."[1]

This is what God has made! And man is doing his best to destroy all these wonders. There is a wise way of bringing low the trees, and there is an unwise way. Alas that in Pennsylvania the unwise and ruthless way usually has been taken. A recent visitor to the valley of the Allies told sorrowfully of finding sawmills everywhere, and of passing six loads of sawed lumber in a distance of seven miles.

Among those who have been guilty of destroying the forests of these valleys was Queen Isabella II of Spain, who, about the middle of the nineteenth century, invested most of her private fortune in timber lands and mining ventures along the West Branch and its tributaries. Her agents built the Fallon House at Lock Haven, which still shelters the traveler, made their headquarters at Farrandsville, and conducted many operations on Quinn's Run and Tangascootac Creek.

For nearly twenty years the royal money was spent

---

[1] From the collected poems of Henry van Dyke. Copyrighted by Charles Scribner's Sons, 1920.

freely in these Pennsylvania fastnesses, but by 1870 the mines were closed, and the lumbering operations were concluded; the disastrous venture was ended.

Yet to this day the traveler who passes through the country under the wing of an old settler is startled to hear him say, as he points to some timbered ridge, "There are some of the Queen of Spain's lands."

CHAPTER XXV

IN EASTERN PENNSYLVANIA

THE traveler in Eastern Pennnsylvania feels himself continually applying to the country through which he passes the words of Sir Walter Scott in the "Fair Maid at Perth:"

"It is long since Lady Mary Montagu, with that excellent taste which characterizes her writings, expresses her opinion that the most interesting district of every country and that which exhibits the varied features of natural scenery in greatest perfection, is that where the mountains sink down upon the Champaign, or more level land. The most picturesque, if not the highest, hills are also to be found in the county of Perth. The rivers find their way out of the mountainous region by the wildest leaps, and through the most romantic passes connecting the Highlands with the Lowlands. Above, the vegetation of a happier climate and soil is mingled with the magnificent characteristics of mountain scenery, and woods, groves and thickets in profusion clothe the base of the hills, ascend up the ravines, and mingle with the precipices."

One reminder of charming Perthshire is the rapid descent from the high ground about Malvern to the Great Valley, and then the great sweep of the valley to the westward, then north, then south to the bounding hills.

The delights of this region were described in 1793 by André Michaux, after his tour of Pennsylvania.

Nine years later he was followed by his son François, who rode through the valley on a day in late June when it was at its best. He crossed the east branch of the Brandywine at Downingtown and the west branch at Coatesville, then passed to Lancaster, where he must have seen the courthouse on Center Square, in which the Continental Congress met for one day, September 27, 1777. This city of the Mennonites, the Amish, and the Dunkards has replaced the historic courthouse by a soldiers' monument, but it still can show many relics of the past along with its evidence of modern progress.

François Michaux went on from Lancaster to Shippensburg, through a country which charmed him at every mile. But great as was his delight in the scenery, it was greater still in his botanizing, especially when he was able to find specimens of the shortleaf pine, a tree that grows luxuriantly farther south, though some specimens may still be found in southern Pennsylvania. The most notable grove of the species, near Mont Alto—perhaps the very grove visited by the French scientist—was preserved by the wise owner, who said, "So long as my eyes remain open these glorious trees will stand." Timbermen eyed with longing the three hundred acres of woodland over which the stately pines towered, but not until 1914 were they able to make their destructive way within the charmed region of the grounds.

Michaux's discovery of the pine trees was commemorated later by the planting of specimens at the Chateau of Fontainebleau, in France, and his keen interest in the trees of the state bore fruit when he left an endowment that enabled the University of Pennsylvania to man the Michaux Lectureship on Forestry.

One of the early holders of the lectureship was Doctor J. T. Rothrock, the father of Pennsylvania's fruitful forest policy, that bids fair to transform what Gifford Pinchot has called "the Pennsylvania Desert," a region larger than the state of New Jersey, where trees have been removed, and where nothing but trees can be made to grow.

Here and there municipalities are following the example of the state by encouraging scientific forestry. Notable among them is Reading, whose efforts to curb the quarrymen who are ruining the best part of Mount Penn have attracted attention. In the edge of the city, above Angelica Creek, two million trees have been planted by the owner of a private estate who invites visitors to climb to a stone observation tower above the forested slopes from which they can look off twenty miles to the Blue Mountains, and can see the Port Clinton Gap.

Reading offers an embarrassing choice of walks and drives that emphasize Bayard Taylor's claim that "few towns on this side the Atlantic are so nobly environed." There is the short trip to State Hill, overlooking the valley of the Tulpehocken, with the Blue Mountains in the distance. There is the climb to the Wernersville heights, overlooking the valley of the Cocalico, with the Welsh Mountains in the distance. There is the varied trip to the hill where Hain's Church peeps down into the Lebanon Valley—the church built in 1766, which still presents above the main door a stone defaced in 1776, when the Declaration of Independence was read to the assembled congregation. Some who heard the words of defiance to King George thought of the legend on the stone, which told of the purpose of

COVERED BRIDGE OVER KISKIMINETAS, NEAR SALTSBURG, PENNSYLVANIA

WEST ENTRANCE TO CALEDONIA PARK, SOUTH MOUNTAIN, PENNSYLVANIA

NIGHT ON PENN STREET BRIDGE, SCHUYLKILL RIVER, AT READING,

the members "to be loyal to the King." The cry was raised, "The King must come out!" A ladder was brought and part of the inscription was removed, and the stone was left with message incomplete. So it is today.

A popular ride is six miles south of Reading to an old stone farmhouse built in 1725, which was the home of Mordecai Lincoln, great-great-grandfather of Abraham Lincoln. Near by is the cabin where the family of Daniel Boone lived. Abraham Lincoln, grandson of Mordecai, and grandfather of the President, married Ann Boone, cousin of Daniel Boone. Later both families emigrated.

The Berks County Conservation Society has provided a series of Travel Trails. One of these, the Antietam Trail, circles Mount Penn, and leads to the City Tree Nursery, at Antietam Lake, then on to Deer Path Hill, where the elevation of one thousand feet permits a wealthy view of portions of the Schuylkill Valley, the Tulpehocken or Lebanon Valley, South Mountain away to the left, and the Blue Mountains to the right. The Allegheny Trail of forty miles has so many points of interest that a folder has been prepared telling of them and describing the route.

Relics of the sturdy settlers among the hills and in the valleys of Berks County are shown in the building of the Berks County Historical Society. Perhaps greatest interest attaches to the plates from old cast iron stoves used by the pioneers.

These pioneers, recent emigrants from central Europe where the cast iron stove, made of plates bolted together, was a customary feature of home life, brought with them to America the taste for this peculiarly made bit of house furniture. At first they imported stoves cast in Europe. Later, when furnaces were opened in America, one of their first products was the plates for these odd stoves. They were called five-plate, six-plate, ten-plate stoves, according to the number of plates in the stove. The early stove had five or six plates, one for each side of the cube into which it was fastened by means of bolts.

The peculiarity of these plates that makes them interesting to present day collectors is that they were marvelously decorated with relief figures, usually representing Biblical subjects. The scarcity of books and papers made this pictorial method of representing Scripture a general favorite.

The method of preparing the plates was very crude. A wooden plate was fashioned, the size of the proposed stove plate. On this was carved in relief the figures and other things which were to be represented, or a relief carving was nailed to the wooden plate. This pattern was then pressed into the moulder's sand and molten iron was poured from the primitive furnace into the pressed sand.

CHAPTER XXVI

WHERE PENNSYLVANIA'S WATERS FLOW

PENNSYLVANIA may not have any coast line —it is the only one of the original thirteen states that does not touch the Atlantic—but it has a wealth of water that distinguishes it even among neighbors richly blessed by lakes and streams. Its lakes are of small account; most of the two score and more are in the northeastern section, though the largest is in the northwestern corner of the state. But the many rivers and countless smaller streams have a peculiar place in the affections of the people, from the Delaware in the east to the Ohio in the west, from the Allegheny and the Chemung on the northern border to crooked Conococheague Creek, tributary of the Potomac on the south. The historian delights in their storied past; the poet feels pleasure in their tuneful names; the traveler rejoices in their beauty that is sometimes quiet and serene, frequently quite spectacular, always dignified; the scientist never wearies of tramping along their banks and asking them to tell their stories of the ages when Pennsylvania was young; while the geographer feels perennial interest in studying the way some of them triumph over the mountains, cutting directly across their great bulk, and the fashion others have of following meekly the valleys between the ridges, borrowing beauty from the overshadowing heights.

Few of the streams are navigable, though the men of the early days were reluctant to own this truth.

How persistently they tried to make the Susquehanna carry their burdens! In 1796 an enthusiast insisted that the prospect of internal commerce on this stream was very bright; he declared that even the Ohio and the Mississippi would have to yield to it because of the extent and value of its commerce. But the shallow waters and the rocks of the Susquehanna at length convinced its partisans of the uselessness of attempting navigation of anything but the canals that were constructed along its banks. These canals were part of a system of internal improvements which may be traced today by relics of their departed grandeur, or they may be mentally reconstructed by those who wander by the artificial waterways still in use, on the banks of the Delaware, the Lehigh and the Schuylkill, for instance.

It is impossible to tell the story of the streams of Pennsylvania without detailing also the romance of the early history of the colony or the state. The southern reaches of the Delaware tell of Penn's friendly dealings with the Indians and of the later proposal to fix the Capital of the United States a few miles above the site of the country home of the founder of the commonwealth, while the more picturesque upper waters speak of pioneers for whom it was a pathway to the wilderness. The Schuylkill, flowing from the region of anthracite, skirts Valley Forge, where Washington performed the miracle of bringing his starving army through a winter of torture. The Susquehanna was the route of those who sought the north, and it floated the rafts of those who went even to Pine Creek and to the Sinnemahoning for the timber that once covered so much of the state. The Juniata and the Conemaugh,

222

WHERE PENNSYLVANIA'S WATERS FLOW

links in the water chain that bound Philadelphia to
Pittsburgh in days before the Pennsylvania railroad,
whisper still the tales of savage uprisings and of surprising escapes, like that of Jane Maguire, who, when
Indians attempted to seize her, took advantage of the
tearing of her gown to jump out of it, and grasp the
tail of a passing cow which, frightened, dragged her to
safety at a fort near the present site of Huntington.

Then there is the Allegheny, which bore Celeron
with his cargo of leaden plates, intended for burial
along the watercourse in token of the claim of France
to the western land, and the Monongahela, favored by
early emigrants to Ohio, which comes up from the south
to join forces with the northern stream in making the
Ohio, the mighty carrier of Pennsylvania's coal to the
valley of the Mississippi.

The stretch of the Monongahela for an air-line distance of thirty-five or forty miles below Pittsburgh is
remarkable for the history that was made there. In
the days of the pioneer who floated down stream from
Redstone Old Fort, near the present site of Browns-
ville, it was noteworthy also because of the picturesqueness of the country through which it flowed. Railroads
and mills, culm banks and coal tipples, clustering
miners' villages and smoky industrial towns have taken
away the beauty for some, though in the opinion of
others the glimpses of industrial Pennsylvania secured
from the banks of the stream add to the attractiveness
of the picture.

Close to the mouth of Redstone Creek the Indians
built their earthworks, and their Anglo-Saxon successors made the first agricultural settlement, probably
about 1750. And to this favored spot, framed in by

223

clustering hills, thousands who sought the West came to begin the adventurous journey by ark or flatboat or keelboat. Primitive boat-building yards were founded there, for the accommodation of those who would trust themselves to the river's hill-bordered trough, where rocky bluffs, broken continually by wooded ravines, led up to the green slopes.

There was boat-building also at the "Forks of Yough," where the Youghiogheny entered the Monongahela. In passing this spot favored by the Indians, pioneers were following in the wake of Major Washington and Christopher Gist, as well as of the ill-fated Braddock, who crossed the Monongahela at the Forks, only to cross again near the mouth of Turtle Creek, hard by the ravine where the French and Indians surprised him. Bustling Braddock covers the site of the massacre, the mills giving prophecy of the clamor and smoke of Pittsburgh.

Towering business structures crowd close to the point where the waters of the Allegheny join those of the Monongahela, but they leave room for the old Block House, built in 1764 by Colonel Bouquet at what has been called "the most strategic plot of ground in colonial days west of the Allegheny Mountains."

In the days when men floated down the river in their flatboats, they liked to stop long enough to climb to the South Side heights, where they could have a satisfying glimpse of the meeting of the rivers and of the hills between. Today the same heights provide vantage ground for modern gazers. For them, however, there is an easier ascent than in those days; they can use the "inclines," which take passengers and freight up the declivities on cars that glide with ease and safety,

224

THE SMOKE AND THE RIVERS AT PITTSBURGH

A BIT OF THE FIVE-MILE RIVER FRONT OF HARRISBURG, PENNSYLVANIA

though to the beginner in Pittsburgh the ride looks
like a questionable venture. But fears are speedily
forgotten as the view unfolds of the city where tall
buildings are near neighbors of smoking stacks and
furnaces belching red flames, where houses cling to
cliffs on which a goat might find delight, where ravines
lead enticingly into the heart of the city, where Schenley
Park provides a home for the great Carnegie Institute,
with its Museum, its Music Hall, its Library School and
its Institute of Technology, as well as for the University
of Pittsburgh, whose founding in 1787 enables it to
boast that it is the oldest institution of learning, except
the University of Nashville, west of the Alleghenies.

The keen satisfaction of those who gaze on the
wonders of the waterways of Pittsburgh cannot be
complete until the journey is continued down the Ohio,
to the Great Bend, and to Rochester and Beaver.
Rounded hills, graceful bends, verdant islands, and
mysterious-looking ravines make the twenty-five miles
so varied that it is easy to wish to make the bend, instead of a terminus, a mere stage in a loving inspection
of *La Belle Riviére.*

But those lower reaches of the Ohio will wait until
the traveler goes to the Delaware and follows its mean-
derings entirely along the eastern border of the State.
The bold navigator from Virginia who passed within
the Capes and marveled at the tawny flood that came
down from the north, did not ascend it far, but he saw
enough of it to decide that it was worthy of bearing
the name of Lord de la Warr, the Governor of the Province of Virginia. He carried back with him surprising
tales of his discovery, but they were nothing to the
stories he might have told if he had been privileged

to ascend the stream to the head of navigation at Trenton, and then one hundred and eighty miles farther to the stretch of river where venturesome canoemen like to begin their journey toward the sea.

It is indeed a venture to guide a canoe from the New York line to Trenton, but every year there are those who decide that it is a venture worth making. The trip provides many thrilling moments when the eye must be glued to the river lest sudden disaster end the journey, just as it offers endless temptations to lift the eyes to the marvels of bordering mountains, islands that are fit to be the abode of the fairies, cascades whose waters meet the rainbow, massive cliffs of formations varied and fantastic.

The upper river flows through a country wild and mountainous, where rocky cliffs look down at one moment on a quiet current, and next instant, perhaps, on a threatening torrent. The miles above Port Jervis are as wild as any river country to be found in the East; one enthusiast who brought his canoe safely through said they would not be unworthy of the Colorado River. He was especially attracted by the country about Lackawaxen, where he dashed through a twelve-foot opening in the dam, making a mad rush that seemed to him to be at the rate of a mile a minute.

Shohola Falls, Mongaup Falls, and Butler Falls are incidents on the way to Port Jervis that add to the danger of canoe navigation, while they help to make the river notable in the eyes of those who seek the beautiful.

The mouth of the Neversink near Port Jervis marks the point where the borders of Pennsylvania, New York, and New Jersey touch. Tri-State Rock is sought by

CANAL SCENE NEAR BETHLEHEM, PENNSYLVANIA

ELEPHANT'S FEET ROCKS, MILL RIFT, PENNSYLVANIA

JUNCTION OF DELAWARE AND NEVERSINK RIVERS

thousands who wish to stand near the boundary, or to climb to the height above which enables the eye to roam far and see wonders that cannot easily be forgotten.

Below Port Jervis the country becomes less rugged for a time; then, forty miles down, the mountains succeed wonderfully in a mighty effort to make the river passage remarkable. They crowd down to the water, Mt. Minisi on the Pennsylvania shore, Mt. Tammany on the New Jersey side. Really, these two are one mountain; somehow during the ages the river has persuaded them to let it through. And now from its surface the traveler looks up the verdure-clad precipices to summits sixteen hundred feet above the sea.

From the Water Gap to the Forks of the Delaware and Easton—where the Lehigh River enters from the west—the Delaware Indians used to paddle their canoes past the wooded islands, dexterously conquering the rafts and rapids that impede navigation. The worst of these, Foul Rift, has cost the lives of many unwary river men.

From Easton to the Falls of the Delaware at Trenton the river flows more quietly. Yet even here there are treacherous rifts as well as banks that lure the wayfarer to brave the dangers while he crosses to study more closely trickling waterfalls, leafy banks or beetling cliffs.

This is the region of the most famous crossing—that of Washington in 1776. And a few miles below the capital of New Jersey is Dunker's Ferry, where, on December 25, 1776, Captain Thomas Rodney took five companies of light infantry, on boats, to the New Jersey shore. They were impeded by the floating ice and chilled by the biting wind. Three hours they remained on the land, compelled to be inactive while they covered the retreat of other troops. Then once more they fought the floating ice as they sought the Pennsylvania shore. Their double passage was as remarkable as that of Washington and his men, but, because they were merely manœuvering to allow others to do great tasks, fame has passed them by.

Not a great distance from Dunker's Ferry is the junction with the Delaware of the beautiful Neshaminy, the stream on whose bank John Fitch was walking when he had his vision of the steamboat that later made regular packet trips between Philadelphia and Burlington.

The banks of the Delaware, from the stretch where the steamboat of Fitch used to ply to the source in New York State, call loudly to the pedestrian as well as to the wise men who favors the canoe. But to those who would see the heart of Pennsylvania while they are following a stream both historic and beautiful the smiling Susquehanna makes appeal even more insistent than does the Delaware. Those who wish to combine the trips in one long, glorious summer holiday have only to leave the Delaware near the northeastern corner of the state and walk a few miles to the spot where the Susquehanna first crosses the line from New York into Pennsylvania. Then comes the loop into New York State, where the river is joined by the Chenango River, coming down from the north and adding to the attractiveness of bustling Binghamton.

Excepting the St. Lawrence, the Susquehanna drains the largest area of all the rivers that enter the Atlantic. Its basin measures 27,000 square miles, most of it in Pennsylvania. Yet it is necessary to travel less than four hundred miles to see the country along most of its length, including the West Branch.

When the Susquehanna enters Pennsylvania the second time, it is in a beautiful valley which narrows to a point where the river receives the waters of the Chemung at Tioga Point. Then comes a succession of hills and valleys which the Indians were reluctant to leave when the pioneers crowded in from the north, the east and the south.

The most famous of the valleys, and one of the most popular with the Indians, as with those who have succeeded them, was the Wyoming Valley, a lingering place for the warriors who were on their way from the St. Lawrence to the Potomac, and the seat of several important villages. These villages sprang up where the trails by which the Indians followed the smaller streams intersected the river. One of these villages, Asserughny, was located near the mouth of the Lackawanna. There the contrast of hill and valley and the supply of fish in the river made constant appeal to the Delawares, who found keen delight in the beauty about them, as well as intense satisfaction in gathering the good things the world provided.

There were other valleys at intervals to the present site of Sunbury, at the junction of the West and North Branches, where Shamokin was located. This was the Indian town which a missionary in 1746 called "the very seat of the Prince of Darkness." But it was a natural paradise. The rivers, the valleys, the boldly encroaching hills, made a picture whose charm can easily be imagined now that nothing is changed but the covering forests.

The West Branch vies with the North Branch both

in wild and varied beauty and in its reminders of the past. There are mountains that touch the waters, as well as many others that make a distant frame for the uplands between. Everywhere are towns and villages which staged romantic episodes of days that are gone. It is difficult to believe that Williamsport was once a rough-and-tumble lumber town, but the charm of river and mountain is increased by the thought of the hardy men who faced the perils of rocks and riffles as they brought out of their mountains great rafts destined for builders in the lowlands.

A landmark of the early navigation of the river was Great Island, near Lock Haven. Today a state road crosses the fertile land which, in 1768, was bought from its Indian owner by a surveyor who gave him, for the 280 acres, his rifle and equipment, as well as a keg of whiskey. When the Indian was sober he tried to buy back the island, but the new owner insisted on his bargain.

Above Great Island Lock Haven stretches picturesquely along the south bank of the river. On the green near the water's edge is the site of Reed's Fort, where, in 1778, the murder of an Indian precipitated the famous "Great Runaway," when the Susquehanna was the scene of excitement unparalleled in its turbulent history. From up river and from tributary waters came a long procession of refugees, seeking safety at the fort below.

Above Lock Haven—which was named because of the lock in the canal and a raft harbor in the river—the valley is now narrow, now broad. The railroad follows the sinuous curves of the stream. The bluffs sometimes rise precipitously from the water, their tree-clad slopes darkening the depths beneath. At times there is a more open space, where, perhaps a highway approaches a primitive rope ferry. Frequently the mountains seem to close in on both sides of the river, as if to make passage impossible. Then comes one of the graceful gaps through which the pioneers moved on to the conquest of the wilderness.

"Wonderful, isn't it?" was the enthusiastic remark of the Pullman conductor on a train that was threading these regions on toward some of the highest land of the state. "I have traveled with parties all over the United States," he added. "I have been to the Grand Canyon of the Colorado and to all the National Parks. But for real satisfaction and endless delight give me the West Branch Valley and the valley of the Sinnemahoning."

Another fellow-traveler declared that his favorite stretch of the Susquehanna was farther south, on the seventy miles of the main river between Sunbury and Harrisburg. "To me it is the finest bit of railway travel in the country," he declared. And it would be difficult to find a more attractive bit of country. As the river flows over its rocky bed there are rapids and eddies as well as still pools. It is studded with green islands; sometimes there are so many of these, at an unusually broad section of the shallow river, that the observer on the bank has a vista that is a reminder of the Highland lochs in Scotland. Beyond the river the ridges rise one above another until the far-away horizon limits the vision. The eastern bank is fringed with vine-covered trees that grow from the bed of the canal where once boatmen guided their narrow craft in sight of Mahantongo Mountain by the side of a great body of dead water which they called "The Irish Sea."

231

Down toward Harrisburg the bank should be deserted for a most distinctive study of mountains and river from midstream. From the great Rockville stone arch bridge on the main line of the Pennsylvania railroad may be seen, on the north, the mountains closing in on the river. while, to the south, the stream, generously broad, makes room for islands fertile and beautiful. Up-river the current is broken by the crumbling arches, reminder of an ill-starred railroad venture of a past generation, which have gradually yielded to the attacks of the ice that grinds down on them with the break-up of winter.

But even better is the vision from the lofty dome of the Capitol building that is the central feature of Harrisburg. It is worth while to toil to this point of vantage, not only for the vision of valley and river and mountain, but for the interior survey of the vast dome, where are displayed the words of William Penn concerning the founding of his colony:

"That we may do the thing that is truly wise and just. . .
"That an example may be set up to the nations. . .
"That there may be room there for such a holy experiment. . .
"For the nations wait a precedent. . .
"And my God will make it the seed of a nation."

From this monumental building, with its two acres of floor space, its bronze doors which Theodore Roosevelt said were the most beautiful he had seen, and its Violet Oakley paintings, the way is short to the banks of the Susquehanna, bordered by the five-mile boulevard, a bower of rich green—a section of the system of parks of which Harrisburg has a right to be proud.

232

WHERE PENNSYLVANIA'S WATERS FLOW

From Harrisburg to the sea the river at every turn discloses fresh reason for satisfaction. It never repeats; it seems never to weary of showing how many things a river can do to charm those who follow where it leads.

The beauty of the Susquehanna appealed to some of the statesmen of 1789 and 1790 so much that they nearly succeeded in fixing on Wright's Ferry, which is now Columbia, as the site of the Federal District and the Capital of the nation. Parton, in his life of Jefferson, tells how the project failed.

"A ring loomed up dimly upon the imagination of members, supposed to have been formed...in order to fix the capital at Wright's Ferry, on the Susquehanna. The members from New England and New York agreed in preferring it, as the point nearest the center of population, weather and convenience, and for many days it seemed to have a better chance than any of the other places proposed—Harrisburg, Baltimore, New York, Germantown, Philadelphia. But Wright's Ferry lost its chance through the opposition of the southern members, and the ring-rumor was the ass's jaw-bone which they used to kill the project. The members from New England and from New York denied the offensive charge, and contended that Wright had fixed his ferry at the point which would be the center of population for ages to come....The Susquehanna men triumphed in the House, but the Senate sent back the bill with Susquehanna stricken out...."

On the river below old Wright's Ferry every mile is notable. These attractions culminate toward Peach Bottom, the proposed terminus of a canal planned in early days between the Delaware and the Susquehanna.

Later a canal was actually built on the York County side
of the river. Now the old tow-path is used for a road-
way, while the bed of the canal has been filled
up by soil washed down from the hills.

Peach Bottom was the name given to settlements
on both sides of the river. The York County village
was an important shipping point. Now nothing is left
of the once busy place but the ghost of an old hotel; the
weather-beaten warehouses by the side of the slip into
which the canal boats passed when about to receive and
discharge cargo; the old saw-mill, with its great wooden
wheel; and the grist mill, where a twenty-five-foot wheel
is fixed in the debris brought down by the rushing tributary stream that supplies the power. The buildings
are falling into ruins—except the roofs, which are
of slate.

Down the river an abrupt hill of solid slate runs to
a height of nearly five hundred feet, the cliff side toward
the river. The climb up the difficult inland slope is
fascinating because of the dense foliage. Then the
view from the summit!

Most of those who come to this favored spot cross
the river from the Lancaster County shore to the York
County slopes on a primitive ferry which is guided by
the captain, who is also the engineer, the fireman, and
the deckhand. After firing the engine, he takes his
stand on the roof and deftly swings the long sweep,
cunningly contrived from a chestnut tree. This sweep
reaches the water beyond the stern wheel. Just at the
feet of the man of many jobs is a hole in the roof which
gives access to the valve controlling the engine.

Fifteen minutes are required for the crossing, for
the river is nearly two miles wide, in spite of the fact

234

that it is above the part where the tide makes itself felt. The course is delightfully crooked, among the rocks and the wooded islands, some low, but many of them quite lofty. The eyes turn lingeringly upstream toward the gap in the hills that tells of secrets hidden there.

Development engineers are casting eager eyes at this section of the river; they would like to drown out the wonderful islands by waters impounded by a great dam. But lovers of beauty hope that the Tucquan Dam—a few miles up-stream—which made a lake of a remarkable bit of river, will be looked upon as development enough for the region.

Back on the Lancaster County side the wanderer may find, hidden among the hills, near the river, another curious water wheel, which once operated the trip-hammer in a primitive edge-tool factory. This wheel is not at the side of the building, but planted on the dirt floor on the inside, where ordinarily the forge would be. As the wheel turned successive cams on the axle tripped the long handle of the hammer, so that it rose and fell to deliver the blows that helped to fashion the tools.

Today few visitors find this bit of country that was once a populous center. A few fishermen know what the river has for them, and there are hunters who make their way there. Rough shacks, as well as a few more ambitious cottages, on the islands and on the mainland, tell of summer visitors who choose to live far from accustomed haunts.

On a day in May the author climbed to the covered porch of one of the plainest of these houses, built of rough boards. At first he thought there was no living thing about. But wait! Where were those two Carolina wrens bound with nice fat worms in their mouths.

Evidently they had a nest near by. But they were wary; for some time they eluded the sharp eyes fixed on them. But at last patience was rewarded; they flew through a knot-hole into the shack. Study of the interior through another knot-hole revealed, after half an hour, a nest within an iron kettle, hung from the rafters. Then came a further reward to the watcher; four fluffy little wrens were helped down from the lofty perch to a mattress rolled up in a corner.

The Peach Bottom neighborhood is famous among lovers of birds. For some reason the migrating birds make their way north by way of the gap in the hills by the Susquehanna. Perhaps they like the trees. Possibly the scarcity of inhabitants appeals to them. Perhaps they do not wish to disappoint the West Chester Bird Club, which makes its annual pilgrimage to the favored spot when the trees are putting on their leaves and it is possible to stroll for an hour or two among the hills or along the river and listen to the clear, liquid notes of birds that sing deliciously, deliriously, ecstatically. In this rich resort for the bird lover as many as one hundred different varieties may be seen or heard during a walk of two or three miles, adding color to the spring landscape in telling their joy that they may be in the glorious forest by the riverside.

INDEX

INDEX

INDEX

INDEX

INDEX

INDEX

INDEX

Rivers: Allagash, 34; Allegheny, 223; Androscoggin, 40; Ashland, 38; Ausable, 151; Black, 157; Brandywine, 196, 217; Charles, 50, 58; Chemung, 229; Concord, 57; Conemaugh, 210, 222; Connecticut, 39, 82, 93; Contoocook, 38; Deerfield, 46; Delaware, 140, 194, 205, 222; East, 140, Elk, 198; Genesee, 171; Green, 75; Harlem, 140; Housatonic, 72, 80; Hudson, 108, 134, 138, 157, 164; Juniata, 210, 222; Kennebec, 18, 33; Lehigh, 222; Merrimac, 37, 38, 54, 57; Mill, 80; Mohawk, 145, 157, 164; Monongahela, 223; Moose, 40; Narragansett, 84; Norembega, 19; North, 140; Ohio, 225; Oswego, 163; Ottagueochee, 47; Pawcatuck, 84; Pemaquid, 18; Penobscot, 19, 27, 31; Piscataqua, 16; Providence, 88; Quinnipiac, 81; Raquette, 157; Raritan, 191; Richelieu, 155; St. Croix, 20; St. Johns, 35; St. Jones, 200; St. Lawrence, 157, 161; Saco, 39, 40, 41; Sagadahoc, 18; Sakonnet, 88; Salmon, 97; Saugus, 56; Schuylkill, 205; Souhegan, 37; South, 140; Sudbury, 59; Susquehanna, 164, 170, 227, 228; Thames, 82; Walloomsac, 45; Wells, 111; Westfield, 72; Westport, 80; Winooski, 112; York, 17; Youghiogheny, 224

Robinson, Pastor, 65

Rochester, New York, 171

Rodney, Captain Thomas, 227

Rogers, Major, and his famous slide, 149

Rome, New York, 168

Roosevelt Memorial Highway, 162

Roosevelt, Theodore, 122, 232

Rothrock, Dr. J. T., 218

Rutgers College, 191

St. Lawrence Reservation, 161

Salem, Massachusetts, 55

Samoset, 18, 19

Sandy Hook, 178

Saranac Lake, 159

Saratoga Springs, New York, 145

Say and Seal, Lord, 95

Saybrook, Connecticut, 82, 95, 96

Schenectady, New York, 164

Schuylerville, New York, 146

Scott, Sir Walter, 216

Sebago, Lake, 33

Shoals, Isles of, 16

Shoemaker, Colonel Henry W., 7, 212

Siasconset, 91

"Skeleton in Armor, The," 87

Slaves freed in Vermont, 153

Sleepy Hollow, 141

Smith, Captain John, 63, 70

Smith College, 104

Snake Hill, New Jersey, 192

Springfield, Massachusetts, 72, 94, 101

Stamford, Connecticut, 78, 79

Standish, Myles, 60, 64, 65, 70

Stanley, Dean, 50

State College, Pennsylvania, 208

Staten Island, 178

Steamboat tested, 109

Stepping Stones, Historic, at Philadelphia, 202

Steuben, General Frederick William, 167

Storm on Lake George, 149

Storm King, 142, 143, 144

Storm bound on Mount Washington, 43

243

INDEX